D0849781

A TRUE MAN OF GOD

A Biography of
Father Ralph William Beiting,
Founder of the Christian Appalachian Project

Father Beiting takes his ministry to the Ohio River.

Courtesy W. Brunner—Berea, Kentucky

A TRUE MAN OF GOD

A Biography of
Father Ralph William Beiting,
Founder of the Christian Appalachian Project

by
Anthony J. Salatino

edited and with a foreword by
Sidney Saylor Farr

The Jesse Stuart Foundation
Ashland, Kentucky
2001

Copyright © 2001 By Anthony J. Salatino
First Edition
All Right Reserved. No part of this book may be reproduced or
utilized in any form or by any means, electronic, mechanical,
including photocopying, recording, or by any information storage or
retrieval system, without permission in writing from the Publisher.

Library of Congress Cataloging-in-Publication Data

Salatino, Anthony J.
   A true man of God : a biography of Father William Beiting, founder of
the Christian Appalachian Project / by Anthony J. Salatino ; edited and
with a foreword by Sidney Saylor Farr.
      p. cm.
   Includes bibliographical references and index.
   ISBN 0-945084-93-5
     1. Beiting, Ralph W. 2. Catholic Church—United States—Clergy—
Biography. 3. Christian Appalachian Project—Biography. 4. Missionaries—
Appalachian Region—Biography. 5. Appalachian Region—Church history.
I. Farr, Sidney Saylor, 1932-II. Title.

BX4705.B2755 S25 2001
282'.092—dc21
[B]

                                         2001038453

Printed in Canada

Published by:
The Jesse Stuart Foundation

Foreword

For more than a century, Appalachia has been an island of poverty in America's sea of plenty. No one has done more to address the problem of Appalachian poverty than Father Ralph William Beiting, President of the Christian Appalachian Project (CAP), an internationally-known relief agency that has made a major impact on Appalachia for almost fifty years. The problems faced by the CAP were born from a combination of unique historical circumstances that began in the middle of the nineteenth century.

The devastations of the Civil War and the post-war political discriminations combined to create intense poverty in Appalachia, and this poverty was magnified by the region's geographical isolation. Often, the only significant contact with mainstream society came during times of war. When Uncle Sam beat the drums, mountain boys marched forth, for they were true patriots. War offered them temporary employment and adventures that were re-told for a lifetime. But, for the most part, Appalachians rarely traveled beyond the confines of their home counties.

The poverty that outsiders "discovered" in the twentieth century was a product, then, of historical circumstances, and not a comment on the character of a great regional people. To address poverty and poverty related problems in the twentieth century, doctors and nurses, school teachers, social workers, and missionaries came from outside the mountains and worked in the area teaching, healing, and converting the people. For example, the Council of the Southern Mountains (CSM) worked in different locations from 1913 - 1970. The CSM worked on various levels to uplift and enhance the lives of Appalachia's poor. In addition, settlement schools and handicraft organizations enjoyed long lasting results in certain areas of the mountains. But the Christian Appalachian Project, founded by Father Ralph William Beiting in the 1950s, has had a profound impact, helping more than a million people annually.

The poverty that Father Beiting and his predecessors addressed was pervasive and uncontained. It had spread and inhabited Appalachia and left an unrelieved, lifelong ugliness and misery that defined the life of many generations of mountain people.

I know Appalachian poverty from personal experience. I am a native of Bell County in Eastern Kentucky. I grew up during World War Two, and my family lived in poverty until I was an adult.

Poverty is of the senses: the smell, sound, sight, feeling, and taste. Poverty is also fear, apathy, and deprivation of the spirit.

It is the smell of cooking grease, used and reused, saturated into clothes and hair and rotting upholstery. It is the sleeping smell of beds crowded with bodies and threadbare blankets. It is the smoking smells of homegrown tobacco rolled into paper cigarettes, and lumps of coal burning in grates or cook stoves. It is the smell of overripe garbage, dust, and heat in summer, cold dampness in winter.

Poverty is a sound. It is the sound of shrieks in the night, and noise all day long: shuffling feet, hacking coughs, insistent leaks and drips and wind blowing through cracks in the house. Poverty is the most constant sound-track in Appalachia.

Poverty is the sight of bowed shoulders, useless hands stuffed into empty pockets, averted eyes; the sight of faces pinched by years of need, guarded, permanently old; the sight is of a junk strewn waste land, or of streets that are a blighted wildernesses of asphalt, brick, steel, and random blowing trash. And it is the raw ugliness of crowded, unscreened, fly-specked rooms, and of faded clothes too large or tight or threadbare for the body they conceal.

Poverty is pain. It is a feeling through the pores, in the belly, on the feet. Cold so sharp it burns and heat so sweltering and aggressive it chills. The feeling of poverty is dull aches, twinges, pangs, brief satisfactions, creeping numbness.

Poverty is the taste of too many starches and too few fruits, stale bread and spoiling vegetables, cheap coffee and soft drinks.

Poverty is fear. It is apathy so total that the body is drained of all but the dullest perceptions, drugged to all but the most primitive hungers; fear of the enormity of demands and lack of energy. The light flickers briefly. This is poverty of the mind.

Then there is poverty of the spirit. This is the most widespread deprivation of all. This is the poverty that afflicts those who have money as well as those who have none. Its need is deeper than flesh and more craving than thirst. It denies the human capacity for empathy and the creative process necessary for imagination.

Physical poverty captured national attention in the 1960s. There were reports which aroused public awareness of the poverty even close to affluent doorsteps. We heard a lot of talk about "pockets of poverty" in the 1960s. In my experience there are no such things. Poverty is like a communicable disease.

"Poverty is fashionable this season," cynics in Washington said as America awoke to both urban and rural poverty.

Impressive investments of time and energy on the part of many people have been channeled into the War on Poverty. Massive amounts of money and energy were mustered to doctor the symptoms.

Early in 1964 a public opinion poll showed that 51 percent of our comfortable middle-class Americans believed that the poverty-stricken people could pull out of their deep trouble if only they wanted to. "Why don't mountain people get jobs and go to work?" they asked. The answer was multi-fold, encompassing geography, isolation, and a lack of training. Many spoke of it, but very few really understood poverty. While many talked about the problem, one special man began to do something about it.

On October 7, 1950, Father Ralph Beiting, a young Roman Catholic priest, began his missionary work in Eastern Kentucky. Growing up during the Depression in Northern Kentucky, Beiting learned frugality and hard work from his parents who had eleven children to support. Their example of putting God first in their lives greatly influenced his life and conduct. As a child he heard about Appalachia's problems and needs.

As a missionary, Beiting's assignment was to serve as pastor of the parish that covered a four county area which was about the size of the state of Rhode Island. He had to start without a church or congregation. In fact, there were just a few Catholics living in this remote mountain country. But other churches resented Beiting's coming in as though no one had been there before. They accused him of trying to steal their own recruits.

Father Beiting found devastating poverty in every community he visited. The story of how he set out in faith with very little money but burning with God's love for the poor people of Appalachia, and his subsequent missionary work, standing by itself, would have been a dramatic biography. But that was only part of the story of what this man dreamed, planned, and brought about for people in poverty.

During his first year as a priest, Beiting began his long journey of bringing spiritual guidance and physical relief to the people of Appalachia. He focused his ministry on meeting the physical needs of the total community.

For those who were in desperate need, he immediately set out to collect food, clothing, and household goods to ease their burden. At first he relied entirely on contributions from his family and friends in northern Kentucky. He soon realized, however, that this was a short-term solution and something more must be done to break the cycle of poverty. Could he become involved at the personal level in an attack on years of neglect? Beiting brought a positive attitude to the challenges ahead.

He was a champion for quality education and believed in fairness to all races. His ideas of excellence, self-discipline, and concern for all people, along with determination and industry reached virtually every community in Eastern Kentucky.

He set out to gain converts for the Roman Catholic Church, to lift up their ambitions, to ennoble their lives. After a few years of work, his faith, and his ideas caught the attention of the Catholic Church nationwide. His missionary zeal and his belief in God's love for all people brought him to attack poverty wherever he found it.

Father Beiting is realistic about the impact he and his workers have had on Appalachia. "We're not the whole answer to overcoming poverty, just a part of it. Other people will stand on our shoulders to reach higher, but they would not have got there if we had not built a strong foundation."

Through five decades of serving, Father Beiting's example

has inspired a nationwide network of faithful donors and volunteers. These people have contributed through financial and in kind gifts, and their support has played an important role in his evangelism.

Ever since he arrived in Appalachia, Father Beiting's love for the region has never wavered. "To love Appalachia," he recently observed, "one has to have a sense of loyalty." That loyalty to a region and its people is the well-told story before you.

Sidney Saylor Farr
Berea, Kentucky

TABLE OF CONTENTS

ACKNOWLEDGEMENTS

EPILOGUE

Courtesy Father Beiting Collection

Msgr. Beiting, his brothers and sisters at a family gathering.

ACKNOWLEDGEMENTS

First and foremost I wish to thank Father Ralph William Beiting for whom this biography is written. Ever since we first met to discuss this book, he has graciously answered every question, and provided documents, published and unpublished material, tapes, films and photographs. Another rich source of information on Father Beiting's life was his sister, Sister Mary Martha Beiting, SND. I cannot express enough appreciation for her selfless assistance in making available an extensive collection of articles, letters and other materials that include parts of diaries. Special thanks to Mary Lou Deavy and her husband, Jim, for welcoming me into their home, serving as hosts and helping to make my interviews with all the other Beiting family members especially worthwhile. They include Rose Beiting (Ray's surviving wife), Donald and Pat Beiting, Pete and Dorothy Noll, Paul and Doris Beiting, Jim and Joan Beiting, Gene and Ann Schadle, Sister Mary Martha, Stanley and Billie Sue Beiting, and Jerry and Rosalie Beiting.

I am indebted to Father Lou Brinker, Father Terence Hoppenjans, Father Herman Kamlage, and Father John Rolf who shared their thoughts and memories about Father Beiting. There are other people who have known Father Beiting since his early years in Appalachia that deserve my gratitude for their reflections and information, such as Jim and Doris Anglin, Dale and Marie Anastasi, Mary Ann Bullock, George and Wanda Purcell, and John Lynch.

My thanks to the staff members of the Christian Appalachian Project who have helped in many ways and provided invaluable comments and insights into Father Beiting's work. Led by President Mike Sanders, they are: J.C. Adams, Bill Begley, Peggy Gabriel, Richard Ginn, Sheila Helton, Kathy Kluesener, Kathleen Leavell, Mike McLaughlin, Moe Mercier, Rose Price, Grant Satterly, Donna Turner, and Brenda Wireman. A special word of thanks is due to Marilyn Stefanski, Father Beiting's assistant, and Jim Haragan, his office manager, for responding to my many phone calls and providing "extra bits of information."

I also wish to thank the following persons who have interacted with me about the impact of Father Beiting's work; Randy and Martha Carter, Connie Maddox, and Tony Turner. Many other people whose names I have not included responded to questions, and I am also grateful to them.

Others who contributed important information to this book and whom I like to thank are: Brother David Richardson of the Department of Archives and Manuscript, Mullin Library, Catholic University; David Schroeder of the Catholic Center Archives, The Diocese of Covington, Kentucky; Sister Mary Kevan Seibert, SND, Chancellor and Archivist of the Catholic Diocese of Lexington, Kentucky; Don Besky, Archivist of the Archdiocese of Cincinnati and the Glenmary Home Missioners.

I should like to acknowledge Sister Karen Burns, OSF, and Charley Smolski who were asked to provide their professional criticism of this work. They did an outstanding job. I am so very grateful to my manuscript typist, Martha Sexton. She did an excellent typing job and has been a stable force throughout the various revisions of the book.

Finally, I would be remiss if I did not thank my understanding wife and my family for their support while writing this biography.

Ralph William Beiting
as a toddler

Courtesy Father Beiting Collection

CHAPTER I

BORN TO SERVE GOD

In examining Ralph William Beiting's life, the following people, events, and experiences were part of countless contributions that molded and helped him grow into his vocation. Family environment and strong Christian values made it possible for Ralph William to find himself and determine his identity at an early age. Also, the religious beliefs of the Beiting family, combined with Catholic teachings, were instrumental in shaping his desire to serve God. As a result, he was highly motivated toward learning and understanding the meaning of Christian community. Living in poverty and its consequences were overcome because of his positive attitude and a sense of determination to achieve.

Ralph William Beiting had an extraordinary way of introducing himself to this world. He was born on New Year's Day, 1924, the first child of Ralph T. and Martha Hiance Beiting from Newport, Kentucky. When Ralph William was a toddler, the family moved into a farmhouse, originally owned by his grandparents, about five miles south of Newport, in Highland Heights. The farmhouse, on eight and one-third acres of land, became permanent home for the Beitings and their growing family, which would eventually include eleven children. Young

Beiting witnessed the love his parents had for each other and for God. He remembers how his father left for work each day.

> *On his way out the door, he never failed to kiss my mother and wish her a good day. After a long day of work, he'd return home. My mother would meet him at the door, and again they'd exchange tender greeting. ...That simple routine was my first impression of love, not just romantic love, but also love of family, and the feeling that we were special to each other—that, in fact, family was love.*[1]

There were many memories of love and family closeness relating to Ralph William's early years. He and his six brothers and four sisters were surrounded by their parents, grandparents, uncles, aunts, and many cousins, who all lived in the immediate area. In this large family he felt safe, loved, and cherished. Due to the size of the Beiting and Hiance clans, his memory for names and faces was trained at an early age, and would be a blessing throughout his life. The Beitings and the Hiances came from Germany. Ralph William's great-grandfather Beiting migrated to the United States with two brothers, and lived in Cincinnati, until settling down in Newport, Kentucky. Grandfather Beiting was one of eight children and had nine of his own, with Ralph William's father being the second oldest. On the maternal side of the family, Grandfather Hiance was born on a ship in New York harbor, while his parents were getting ready to land on Ellis Island. Ralph William's mother was one of seven children to Grandfather and Grandmother Hiance, who settled in Fort Thomas, Kentucky.[2]

Growing up in a home full of warmth, practicality, and intense religious beliefs provided Ralph William and his broth-

Ralph William with Ray, Don, and Dorothy at an early age.

ers and sisters with a strong foundation. His parents committed themselves totally to their church, showing openmindedness and respect for the views of others. They were staunch Catholics, and on the day of their marriage, both prayed for a large family. Years later, Ralph William asked his parents why they had so many children. He was told that they wanted to be a part of God's kingdom, and felt that life was the greatest gift. They were not afraid of a challenge, conflict, or sacrifice, and wanted their children to be taught from the beginning that God was the reason for everything.[3]

When Ralph William was five, he was enrolled at St. Joseph Catholic school, located on the grounds next to the parish church in Cold Spring, Kentucky. One of the most cherished responsibilities for young boys in a Catholic school was to help the priest by serving daily Mass. Beiting was very eager to be an altar boy. Excitement of the first conscious plunge into doing something for God had built a strong desire in him. He and a close friend, Bill Klump, began to pester Sister Jullitta, who was in charge of the altar boys. Since they were in the first grade, she told them that this could only take place at the third grade level, and to wait until that time. However, Ralph William and his friend kept bothering Sister Jullitta until she finally talked to the pastor who made an exception to the rules.[4]

Beiting's altar boy experiences proved beneficial. His first plunge into doing something for God ignited a life long passionate attachment to the church and strong devotion to God. It was about this time that people asked him what he would like to be.

> *I told them I was going to be the Pope. ...I don't know why I said that, except the Pope seemed to be the best there was. ...Naturally, a little boy wanted to be as good as he could be, and so I skipped the priesthood, along with all the steps in between and simply wanted to be the Pope.*[5]

Young Beiting was well liked by everyone. He was good-humored, outgoing, and always set his sights high. Even at this early age, he believed that service to God was the greatest aspiration anyone could have. His parents made the foundation for that feeling, which they reinforced at the dinner table each evening. They often talked about members of the family who did good deeds for others, which exemplified their unselfishness. Years later, Beiting reflected on this intrinsic goodness of the entire clan:

*My parents, grandparents, aunts and uncles—the
entire family—were dedicated to the idea that love
given to you should be given to someone else.*[6]

As Ralph William began his second year at St. Joseph Elementary School in 1929, the Great Depression reared its ugly head, stunning middle class Americans. With the Depression, people lost their jobs, homes, or both. The Beiting clan was no exception to the unemployment picture. Before the Depression, Grandfather Beiting and his eight sons worked in construction as carpenters and bricklayers. However, during this devastating economic period, constructing new houses and buildings came to a standstill. Lack of job opportunities led to the layoff of Ralph William's father, uncles, and grandfather, as they joined the unemployed. To sustain the daily needs of every family member, the Beiting clan's resources drained away. This was devastating, but they all resolved to work together to overcome the bad times. They had a passionate faith in God and were willing to sacrifice for their loved ones.[7]

These distinguishing traits of the Beiting family generated a memory that would leave a deep impression on Ralph William. Years later, in his own book, *Dreams of Faith*, he wrote with pride:[8]

*Though my formative years were passed in the very
depths of the Depression and my family was poor, I
can't recall a crisis when we ever felt alone, or unable to cope. The reason was family. When one family member was in trouble, the others pitched in.
There wasn't any begging. You hardly had to even
ask for a hand, usually it was offered before you
asked. No one felt beholden to anyone else because*

you repaid your debts by helping the next family member who needed help. My family wasn't perfect...there were certainly arguments, and turmoil was not unknown...but we overcame our difficulties together. I've always felt that God has meant for us to live as one big family.

In the early Depression years, Ralph William's father, an excellent carpenter, was unable to find steady employment so he depended on odd jobs. With a growing family to support, Ralph T. Beiting eventually accepted work through the Works Project Administration. People were employed in WPA projects that included construction of schools, hospitals, and government buildings which allowed them to keep their dignity by performing useful services rather than accept welfare grants.

Hard work was a way of life for Ralph T. Beiting, as he labored from dawn to dusk for a meager income. After dinner, he packed a suitcase full of Watkins Household Products, hoping to earn a little extra money by selling door-to-door in Newport and surrounding communities. Ralph William remembers the look of quiet determination on his father's face as he went out the door each evening.

Poverty during the Depression was so great that people suffered indignities they never dreamed of having to endure. On one such occasion, the age of innocence suddenly ended for young Beiting. He and his parents were on their way home from visiting two of his younger brothers in a Cincinnati hospital. To get home, they had to drive over a toll bridge, spanning the Ohio River. As they approached the tollbooth, Ralph William was shocked to see his father pass without stopping, and shouted, "Wait, you forgot to pay the dime!" His father said nothing, although his head drooped a bit. Finally, Mrs. Beiting turned around with gentleness, covering up her anxiety, and said: "Son, be quiet. We don't have a dime."[9]

Ralph William Beiting began to understand the power of poverty. He realized how ashamed and hurt his father must have felt about this incident, for he took pride in being a law-abiding citizen. Mr. Beiting was a strong and caring man who made numerous sacrifices for the family's collective and individual welfare. His deep affection for his children, and priority to make sure they had hospital care was difficult to argue. But in spite of having so little, the family made the best of each situation.

Ralph T. Beiting was a survivor, and as the hard times continued, he persevered. Being employed by a government program did not give him satisfaction. He was not alone in his feelings, for most men considered it humiliating to work for the WPA.[10] To him it felt even more painful, since he was always striving to become independent. With the help of Grandfather Beiting, who also could not find work, they borrowed money to go into business raising chickens.

Unfortunately, a fire destroyed the business. With destruction of the chicken farm, the Beitings lost their investment, and hardship and turmoil prevailed. However, through determination Mr. Beiting was able to find employment at a county work project. The need to provide for a growing family played an important role in his later decision to make greater use of the farm land. He and Grandfather Beiting borrowed money once more for a down payment on a cow and some pigs. In addition, the family developed a good-sized vegetable garden, and fruit trees. During canning time, Martha Beiting and her daughters preserved foods for the winter, and made jams and jellies.

The overwhelming part that Ralph William's mother played

in his formative years is obvious.[11] Martha Beiting was a woman of religious conviction, dedicated to her husband and children, and often sacrificed for her loved ones. When Mrs. Beiting expected her fifth child she encountered complications during the pregnancy. One day, Ralph William's father came home early from work, and shortly thereafter the doctor arrived. Martha Beiting had hemorrhaged and appeared to be in great danger of losing the baby. Within a matter of minutes the parish priest and a visiting missionary were at the house. As both clergy prayed at her bedside, the missionary blessed Mrs. Beiting with the Relic of St. Paul of the Cross.

Martha overcame the danger and a baby boy was born a few weeks later. Because of the blessing, his parents named him Paul. The doctor told Mr. and Mrs. Beiting that he wasn't sure if Martha's health could withstand the physical demands of bearing another child. However, they were blessed with six more children.

Mrs. Beiting and her husband had great respect for life and wanted to share God's blessings with their offspring. Martha's strong character was evident in her children's upbringing, as she taught them to be responsible and self-dependent, which became their way of life. "She taught us boys to cook, do laundry, as well as sew and crochet. That may not seem remarkable, but in those days, it was," Ralph William remembers. "We learned to care for babies and small children. Finally, she taught us that we were not lesser men because we mopped floors or cooked."[12]

Mr. and Mrs. Beiting treated each child with respect, and taught them to do the same with one another. The children's values, moral codes, identity, and character were influenced by their parents' loving care. Ralph William (also called Bill), followed by Ray, Don, Dorothy, Paul, Jim, Ann, Martha, Stanley,

Jerry and Mary Lou, learned at an early age that certain things were scarce, or they would have to do without. Yet, in spite of the many handicaps of being poor, this was a family in which the children, by necessity, played a major part in each other's lives, spending a great amount of time together.

Assuming responsibility gave the Beiting children an opportunity to use their physical, social, and emotional capabilities in a positive way. Caring, concern, communication, and commitment marked the formative years, affecting their mental growth and development. Ralph William reminisces with great affection about his brothers and sisters:

> *I think, after my life and Catholic faith, the greatest blessing that has ever been given to me is the fact that I was one of eleven. I feel that people don't fully realize what a large family does in the way of helping form and fashion a member of it. I know full well that I could never have done what I accomplished over the years, had it not been for my brothers and sisters. I don't mean that's because we always loved and cared for each other, we fought with each other too. ...We got mad at each other and we did all the other things that kids do. But through it all we really and truly grew to be a strong family, and one was an inspiration to the other, one was a challenge to the other.[13]*

Looking back at those Depression years, Ralph William Beiting realized how his life as a child was based on a moral structure that embodied family commitment to God. He and his brothers and sisters were provided with opportunities reinforcing independence, responsibilities, and the benefits of being good Christians. As they became older, homogeneity of purpose in daily life grew stronger. Most important to them were family, church, and school, upon which their personal and social relationships evolved.

At that time, Ralph William had a greater awareness of the importance of the church than most children, and it created a definite influence in shaping his life.[14] He did not think of God as being isolated or sequestered in the realm of St. Joseph's Church only, but present in his family, school, and surroundings. In many instances, the church's role was more than spiritual. The demands of poverty during the Great Depression created all kinds of needs, and people looked to the church for help. Its humanitarian efforts of helping the downtrodden left an imprint on Ralph William. Many times, the Beiting family, was called upon to help others in need.

> *During those dark years, there was always a pile of coal beside our house. It was paid for by our parish priest, who offered it to any family that needed it for heating or cooking. We never used any of that pile for ourselves, but every day my father and I would help others load the coal into buckets to take home. ...When I asked my father why we were doing this, he said, "Because it's the right thing to do. Don't worry, we're getting paid by knowing we did good."[15]*

An important influence during Ralph William's elementary school years was his third grade teacher, Sister Jullitta, SND. Through her, he discovered spiritual joy, as well as strong intellectual curiosity and his first real taste of the call to serve. Sister Jullitta, a warm and caring person, always encouraged the children to learn more, and read to them during recess or after school. Some children were not very receptive, and asked why they should participate. Sister Jullitta's response was clear and concise, "Because you'll learn an important trade, the skill of reading and speaking well. By learning these skills, you'll be able to be of service to others." Sister Jullitta gave new direction to the sense of Christian duty by constantly stressing that it was service to others that counted. This did not have an immediate impact on Beiting, but eventually, he answered the call to serve, remembering Sister Jullitta's emphasis on responsibility to others.[16]

While attending St. Joseph's School, Ralph William's interest in sports was an integral part of his young life. This was understandable, since his father had played semi-professional baseball in the Newport-Cincinnati area. When Mr. Beiting managed teams for St. Joseph's Parish Holy Name League, his sons were avid participants and excelled in this sport. By the time Ralph William entered the fifth grade, he became an outstanding shortstop on his father's team. His interest in baseball now overshadowed the desire to be pope.

> *I had selected the name Robert for a Confirmation name and the sisters seemed to be very pleased with that. ...They wanted to know if I chose the name after Robert Bellermine, the priest...or what particular saint I had in mind. I told them that I picked out the name of the manager of the Cincinnati Reds, Bob Hutchinson... and I wanted to be a ball player."* [17]

The enthusiasm for baseball spurred Ralph William and his brothers to participate in the American Legion League in their adolescent years. They enjoyed sharing one another's athletic abilities as comrades in arms.

As the Beiting children played together, they also worked in tandem.[18] Their roles and responsibilities as members of the family reinforced the closeness that existed throughout the childhood years. The experience of working on the farm and doing all the other chores made them supportive and dependent on each other. As a practical matter of survival during the Depression, the children had to find work. In those days, part-time opportunities existed by working on large farms in the area that sold products to the public market in Cincinnati. Ralph William and his brothers and sisters walked miles to these farms and made money by picking berries. If they were lucky enough to fill four carriers (16 quarts), the youngsters earned a dollar. After the berry season they worked for one dollar a day, bringing in hay, or hoeing the various crops. The Beiting children were aware of the struggles in life and knew that they had to contribute to their family. They cherished the fact that the money they gave their mother helped buy food and other necessities for the household.

One of Ralph William's greatest delights was his close relationship with Grandfather Gus Beiting.[19] He was a gentle, hardworking man, whose kindness and giving carried forth throughout the family. Every day, Gus walked a good mile and a half from his house in Fort Thomas to work on the Beiting farm. Ralph William had great respect for his grandfather, and the day-to-day contact helped shape his character. He found Grandfather to be a significant mentor. Gus Beiting was an extraordinary individual, who never had a great deal of book learning, although his fascination for reading was remarkable. Ralph William gained a solid foundation of knowledge from Grandfather, who loved to tell his grandson the things he read about the church and history in general. These stories led Ralph William to develop his own fascination for history and reading that he maintains to this day.

Later in life, when Ralph William was studying at the seminary, a priest who had shown interest in his knowledge of church history asked him:

> *"You certainly know a lot of church history. ...You must have had a good course in high school." I told him that we didn't have a course in high school at all and I learned this from my grandfather, who told me all these things that he had read...and I would remember them.*[20]

As Ralph William progressed through St. Joseph to the eighth grade, he received the religious training and discipline for which parochial schools are known. He also read extensively on his own, building historical knowledge, especially of the Church and its saints. At school, his spontaneity often collided with the realities of St. Joseph's structure and discipline. He was mischievous at times, got into trouble and was sent to the principal's office. Once, Sister Cyril, the principal, told him: "Your fighting will lead to a life that could take you down the road to the reformatory."[21]

As the oldest child in his family, Ralph William had shouldered heavy responsibilities at school. His brothers and sisters looked up to him and he also gained respect among fellow students. Yet, he became a target of example by the nuns. Beiting was strong-willed, yet easy-going—a nurturing person for his younger brothers and sisters. When the school day ended, the boys engaged in their normal after-school fun, which would lead to a variety of practical jokes and mischief. This carried over when they got home, which exasperated their father. But to Mrs. Beiting, her boys could do no wrong.[22] As Ralph William grew older, he learned to channel his assertiveness toward solving problems of daily living. His starting point for maturity came at the next level, his high school years, where he would shine academically.

Students entering Newport Catholic High School had to take an entrance examination. There were certain questions on the test Ralph William did not know how to answer, or had reservations about. He went to the priest who administered the test and explored these questions with him. His inquisitiveness about relationships between facts and ideas impressed the clergyman very much, who felt that this youth had great potential, and said, "I think we'd be happy having you." This priest, Leo Kampsen, would become a friend and advisor to Beiting throughout his high school years.[23]

On school days, Ralph William got up very early for breakfast, milked the cow, helped his brothers take care of the pigs, then went on to school. He was a familiar sight on Highway 27, between Highland Heights and Newport, carrying a knapsack on his back, hitchhiking seven miles to and from school. There was no money for a bus ride, and it was too far to walk, so the alternative was to hitchhike.

Those first days at Newport Catholic were among his most intensive and memorable ones during high school. Along with the excitement of being in a new setting, he experienced anxiety, confusion, frustration, and many jumbled feelings. However, Beiting found an interesting group of a half-dozen priests on the faculty, whose overall approach was to challenge students to strive toward meaningful goals. This made him focus on his work with enthusiasm.

I began to see the wonderful things they were doing...we got to communicate with the priests on a one-to-one basis...they were real people and more

*importantly became our friends...this made a deep
impression on me that clergy could be this way...they
were not simply people at the altar, but did other
things that were good and wonderful as well. ...We
had all kinds of priests, some were funny, others
tough, there were brilliant ones, and a few were ag-
gravating.*[24]

The priests at Newport Catholic High were responsible for
their own parish churches, along with teaching six hours a day.
"We saw a spirit of dedication, since they didn't have to do this,"
Beiting said. "But they came to teach and made it possible for
young people, such as myself, to receive solid educational experiences that encompassed a strong religious foundation. It
was exciting to see people willing to sacrifice."

The diocesan bishop was not too fond of this new school,
and had shown greater preference to the long established Latin
School at Covington, Kentucky. However, the religious staff who
administered and taught at Newport Catholic committed themselves to improve the educational program. There was a certain spirit of the underdog. They wanted students to have meaning in their lives, and Ralph William remembers it as a time
when he and others strove for excellence, devoting themselves
to achieve a goal that seemed impossible.

A year before Beiting entered high school, the bishop or-
dered Newport Catholic to disband its football program. This
seemed unfair, because the school had bought uniforms and
the team was a great drawing card for the kids. He recalls that
in spite of the constraints placed on them, a true sense of unity
prevailed throughout the student body.

It seemed to us students that since those uniforms

were available, they should be used. I don't know who initiated it, but somebody said, let's start our own team, and just go out to play against whomever we can. There were fifteen of us on this team, and we gave our all to play...working and sharing together, we could defy all logic and work marvels.[25]

They organized a football team, and though the boys were without a coach, this did not put a damper on their competitiveness. It spurred them on to try harder. They assembled at the high school field and selected a team captain. Through concentrated scrimmages and developing their own plays, they scheduled seven games with other high school teams in the area. They strove for excellence on their own, winning every game that year except one. Being able to reach high goals and set standards of conduct gave meaning to Ralph William.

It was through pride that we continued to play this sport. ...It was kind of outlawed and we were sort of underground, but that made it even more exciting. ...It was the whole spirit by which we were battling the odds...fighting against the establishment knowing that it did not have to be this way. ...We were able to achieve through sacrifice, energy, determination, and accomplished something very special. I believe that was what we were all about. ...And that was one of the characteristics of this school. ...It was felt that maybe we weren't the apple of this bishop's eye, but nevertheless, we were going to be an important factor in the life of the church, and in our own lives as well.[26]

For Ralph William Beiting, athletics comprised only one facet of his idea of a well-rounded student with the ability and motivation to become a winner. At the end of the first semester, Father Leo Kampsen asked him if he liked his academic progress. Beiting had ranked tenth in a class of forty-one for the grading period, and gave a favorable response. The stern Father Kampsen countered with a statement that shocked his pupil. "Well, I'm going to see to it that you really and truly achieve in this place...would you be willing to do what I ask of you? ...if you don't, and continue goofing off, I want permission to use the paddle on you."[27]

Father Kampsen thought that Ralph William was an exceptional talent, and saw no reason why he couldn't strive for the highest goals of excellence. When Beiting left Kampsen's office, he realized that his efforts were not enough and made a conscious assessment of himself. Because of this lesson, he never forgot the importance of always trying for greater heights.

> *Whenever I start to think I've done well, and I try to pat myself on the back too much, I remember Father Kampsen who called for better deeds.*[28]

Ralph William knew he could do better, even though many times he went to his mentor's office to receive a few "whacks." Kampsen impressed on him that doing good was better than getting swatted. With common sense and persistence, he approached his studies, more motivated by reaching for higher goals. He established a plan of action, fulfilling it through commitment, hard work and ingenuity. At the end of his freshman year, he ranked second in his class.

With each succeeding year, Beiting was ready, willing, and able to accomplish the goals he set for himself.[29] Any sense of insecurity he may have had during his first days at Newport Catholic was replaced with understanding, confidence, and high standards that led him to the pinnacle of academic success and greater religious insight. Ralph William Beiting ranked as the top student of his class in the sophomore, junior, and senior years.

When he became a junior, his plans for the future were well established. He wanted to be an architect, affected chiefly by his family's occupation in construction. The Beitings' positive attitudes and work ethic were a conditioning process that influenced him as well. He enjoyed constructing facilities and felt a sense of pride in designing buildings. It was also fascinating to him, seeing something come out of the ground that was not only utilitarian, but beautiful. There was another reason, probably as important, why Ralph William found architecture interesting. He wanted to accumulate the highest grade average in four years and graduate as valedictorian, which would qualify him for a full scholarship at Xavier University in Cincinnati. In turn, this would lessen the burden of financial hardship for his parents.

Openness and understanding were important to a successful student-teacher relationship. At this time, Father Kampsen encouraged Beiting to consider the seminary. "Instead of wanting to design buildings, I think you ought to form lives. You should be a priest." At first Ralph William was not very receptive, but he agreed to pray and see what God wanted.

One day, Father Kampsen came fifteen minutes late to class, which was quite unusual. He explained to his students that he had received a call to help a man who was in jail because of drinking charges. To make things worse, this person neglected to take care of his wife and five children. As the semester wore on, Kampsen kept his class up to date on the situation. The dedication of Beiting's mentor, who told how he counseled the poor man and his family to eventually overcome their many obstacles, impressed him. The family could have fallen apart, but, through Father Kampsen's guidance, they were able to pull together and move on with their lives. This situation reinforced Beiting's feelings about helping people, and he began to think more about entering the seminary. [30]

At the beginning of his senior year, Father Kampsen told Beiting that he had arranged for him to interview with the diocesan Bishop Francis W. Howard, and asked if there were any objections. "What can I lose?" Ralph William responded. "I'm thinking seriously about going to the seminary."

Bishop Howard was a good man who preferred Covington Latin School over Newport Catholic. In the interview with Beiting, the bishop said, "I've been going over your record and you've done well in that school...but I see you haven't had any Greek. ...I don't know how in the world you'll ever make it in the seminary without having studied this language...however, I am going to give you a chance..." [31]

One of the faculty members at Newport Catholic, Father Rupert Metzler, volunteered to teach Beiting Greek.[32] In his last year of high school, he arrived a half-hour early each day so that Metzler could tutor him. The dedication of Father Metzler further impressed Beiting, and by that time, he had made up his mind to enter the seminary and become a priest. To this day, he says that his entering the priesthood could not have come about without the caring and concern of the clergy from Newport Catholic High School.

If one had to sum up Ralph William Beiting at this stage, his life entailed an endless pursuit of goals. He spent every minute of his daily existence meeting the challenges he faced. When he finished his daily chores in the morning, he hitchhiked to

Newport and attended Mass before school started. After classes, he worked from 2:30 to 6:00 in a grocery store to help support his family, then hitchhiked home, did evening chores, and burned the midnight oil studying his assignments. "It was a full life," he says.

By the time he graduated from high school in May of 1941, Ralph William Beiting had earned many honors and awards. He was valedictorian of his class, won the science award, achieved great religious insight that resulted in receiving the religion award, and strived for excellence on the school's debating team and in elocution contests. Beiting felt fortunate having attended Newport Catholic High, and looked forward to studying at St. Gregory Seminary in the fall of 1941. On graduation day, he visited Father Leo Kampsen who said to this proud young man:

> *I guess you think you've done pretty good. Well, you still didn't do what you could have done...and I want you to leave this school realizing that you've got to do the best that's in you, not just enough to get by or win an award. If there's a challenge you must meet it and excel...not for any other reason except that that's what God expects. He didn't give you those talents and that ability to waste them or to see them unused, he gave them to you to do the best you can."*[33]

CHAPTER II

PREPARING FOR THE PRIESTHOOD

Ralph William Beiting's life during his eight years of required seminary study was a time of many tests on his vocational calling. This was also the formation period when inner resources and strength of character were further molded, refined, and exposed to a more extensive enlightenment of the world. Having gained a greater understanding of Christ and His gift of salvation and love became a constant reminder to Beiting's ultimate aspiration. He wanted to serve Christ with totality, and what better way than through priesthood.

Starting in August 1941, Beiting spent his first four years as a candidate for priesthood at St. Gregory's Seminary in Mount Washington, Ohio.[1] St. Gregory, run by the Archdiocese of Cincinnati, proved to be a very influential experience. Rigors of the daily schedule called for great determination, as seminary life was characteristic of seclusion, dedication, austerity, self-discipline, and self-giving. Beiting became totally immersed in the world of the spirit and details of spirituality. Years later, he said:

> *Seminary life was strictly a matter of study and discipline and trying to catch the spirit of sacrifice that*

would be involved in priesthood. In those days...it was not difficult for us to accept, because everything in the world that we had known involved sacrifice and helping others, and not being too concerned about oneself. I found the seminary to be a wonderful place. ...I was attracted first of all to the opportunity of growing closer to God.²

To Beiting, community life in the seminary was very special, but in the beginning of his freshman year, he and a few others from the bluegrass rural country "were looked down upon as Kentucky hillbillies," he recalls. "At any rate, one was quick to make friends because you became accepted by what you were and what you could do, rather than where you came from." Community spirit was deep, and to this day, more than five decades later, Ralph William Beiting still has close friends he made during those years.

Beiting did well scholastically and his intellectual brilliance gained him recognition, as God blessed his labors in many ways. In other things, such as singing, he was less successful. With a jovial sense of humor, he tells about an experience:

As we entered the seminary, everyone had to audition for the choir. ...Singing, of course, was a very essential part of the liturgy...Father DeDeo, a fine Franciscan priest, unfortunately felt that mine and three other fellows' musical abilities would disrupt the good sounds of the choir. ...We were invited to play handball while the choir rehearsed. ...Well, I became a very fine handball player, but never made the choir or anything that resembled producing good music in church. ...And to this day, I can understand

fully why I was not invited to be a part of the choir.
...Everytime I sing, people look at me as if they want
to pray. ...It was a wise decision on the part of Fa-
ther DeDeo.[3]

In 1941, the world situation was getting severe. War had spread to all of Europe and most of Asia. Then on Sunday, December 7, 1941, Japan attacked Pearl Harbor and our nation was at war. Beiting and his fellow seminarians talked of fighting for the United States, but divinity students were exempt from service. However, Ralph William felt unfulfilled, because he was not able to serve in the armed forces as did his younger brother, Ray.

An important part of Beiting's training was daily Mass. He had always been a firm believer in the Eucharist. His parents deeply involved Christ in their lives, and through a strong faith, they imparted the importance of Mass to the children. They also encouraged them to put into practice what they learned, and use the graces they received in the liturgies. In the seminary, Beiting began to have an even deeper appreciation of what Mass was all about.

I realized how deeply involved Christ was in our
lives...how He loved us so much that He not merely
came to be with us for a time, but always...we could
still touch Him, kneel in His presence, and offer that
same sacrifice of the last supper to His father...it
empowered us to make God aware that nothing else
on this earth mattered to us, other than the holy sac-
rifice that Christ made of Himself. So the Eucharist
became extremely important to me, and the Mass
was more than just simply prayers and sermons, it

was sacrifice, it was the real meaning of what love was all about.[4]

A significant spiritual inspiration during Beiting's first years of seminary life was his growing devotion for the Blessed Virgin Mary. The Holy Family played an important part for his own family even before he entered the seminary, and praying to the Mother of Jesus was a daily routine. During this time, he became acquainted with an upperclassman, Alvin Zugelter, who took young Beiting under his wing and shared thoughts and devotion to the Blessed Mother. Zugelter, who later became a priest in the Archdiocese of Cincinnati, introduced him to St. Louis Marie Grignon de Montfort's writings, which included the treatise, "True Devotion to the Blessed Virgin." This special work of de Montfort's fostered a deep faith of the Blessed Mother's importance in Ralph William Beiting's total commitment to Christ.

> *...The whole concept of my devotion was her tremendous asset in our struggle to become likened to Christ. If there was anyone who knew Jesus and what He was like, it was Mary. She spent her life doing things to promote the cause of Christ. Through the Blessed Mother, I would gain a deeper knowledge of Jesus and a deeper sense of service to Him. That sense of true devotion has remained deep within me over the years. It was one of those discoveries that I would make in the seminary, and the hope of sharing that enthusiasm and love with others as well.*[5]

In his final year at St. Gregory seminary, Beiting wrote a catechism book concerning true devotion to Mary, the Mother of Jesus, in the form of questions and answers. A number of years after his ordination, the missionary congregation of the Montfort Fathers published Beiting's book and distributed it throughout the world.[6]

Ralph William Beiting's classes represented a broad Liberal Arts curriculum that emphasized different types of subject matter. English Literature, namely William Shakespeare, was one of his favorite studies. Beiting had an insatiable literary appetite, and the books that appealed to him the most were those that stood the test of time. He was enamored with works by authors like Joseph Conrad and Hilaire Belloc that dealt primarily with historical topics, such as when the reformation divided Christendom. Beiting's love and patriotism for the United States were evident in his extensive reading about Colonial America and all the things that went into its discovery and formation, especially Kentucky. He also liked literature that helped nourish and strengthen his spirituality. His most rewarding spiritual readings were about the lives of saints. He learned a great deal from the men and women in these stories, who showed extraordinary love for God and dedication to their fellow people.[7]

During his training at St. Gregory, a sense of evangelization came over Beiting. He was always searching for greater horizons of understanding the whole of humanity, especially in Appalachia. Studying about Eastern Kentucky led him to become more interested in mission work.

Beiting's outlook was further shaped by his experience with Father Howard Bishop,[8] who came from Maryland to form a religious community for missionaries, under the auspices of Archbishop John T. McNicholas of Cincinnati. Father Bishop organized the Glenmary Home Missioners of America to meet the urgent need of providing Catholic priests for communities in the U.S. without resident clergy.

In evangelizing an area, the Glenmary Home Missioners established a church, then left it in the hands of a diocese and moved on to other priestless communities. The missions also served as emergency relief centers for the distribution of food and clothing to needy people. In certain farming areas, where individuals wanted to improve their skills in upgrading agricultural situations, the priests cooperated with government agencies to promote more efficient methods. This approach to evangelizing left Beiting with a lasting impression.

Even though a close friend of his, Bob Bersen, became a Glenmary Missioner, Beiting did not join the order.[9] He felt that the Diocese of Covington, which included Eastern Kentucky, had a similar challenge. "Faced with the same enormity of problems and by working in my own home ground, I could do the equivalent through the diocese" he said. "Yet, the Glenmarys were certainly a part of my early formation, and to this day I respect their far-reaching missionary work."[10]

During Holy Week, it was customary for the Diocese of Covington to invite seminarians to meet with Bishop Francis W. Howard and discuss the many aspects of their chosen vocation. Bishop Howard, himself a strong advocate for helping the less fortunate, emphasized to the seminarians the need for missionary priests in Appalachia. Beiting, who admired the bishop's love for the missions, also remembers his efforts.

I will always recall our annual meetings with the Bishop. His concern for the people of Appalachia was constantly on his mind and he wanted us also to be concerned. This was unusual, because in those days the Appalachian mission area of the diocese was known as an ecclesiastical Siberia. You were sent there if you "fouled up" in some fashion in northern Kentucky, or didn't fit in well.[11]

Bishop Howard's determination to share the Catholic faith in the mountain region coincided with Beiting's own enthusiasm about evangelization, and his desire to work in Appalachia. Consequently, a bond of understanding developed between them, which sadly ended when Bishop Francis W. Howard died in 1944. He left a strong impact on this seminarian, who in turn would make his own impression on the people of Appalachia.

As Ralph William Beiting prepared to leave St. Gregory's in June 1945, his training was indelible. The foundation established at the seminary had prepared him for deeper studies at the next level. As an exemplary student, he received a Bachelor of Arts Degree with honors conferred by the Antheneum of Ohio, the Catholic Educational College Network of the Archdiocese of Cincinnati.[12]

Beiting's outstanding work in St. Gregory's seminary led to a smooth transition of study at Mt. St. Mary of the West in Norwood, Ohio. Beiting credits St. Mary's for broadening his horizons. "We no longer had students only from Kentucky and Ohio, our base now extended to other parts of the midwest and northeast," he said. "It expanded my whole concept of what the church was like in other parts of our country."[13]

Competing with other top-ranking seminarians, Beiting excelled in an advanced course of study, concentrating on St. Thomas Aquinas' whole range of philosophy and theology, relating to the problems and needs of society. It was very evident that Aquinas' totality of truth provided great value to Ralph William Beiting, who had gained a deeper understanding of the real meaning of religious life and the events that unfolded before him.

Overall, Mt. St. Mary was a forum from which Beiting's social-spiritual thoughts were further refined. It also reinforced his belief that the Catholic Church was not only concerned with liturgy and the teaching of morals and dogma, but with serving the poor. It was a broadening experience, as he learned of the responsibility to care for others, which went hand in hand with the doctrinal absolutism:

We had to be sharers of God...and do things that were going to benefit all the people—be a servant church. [14]

During Beiting's first year at Mt. St. Mary of the West, the Most Reverend William T. Mulloy became Bishop of the Covington Diocese. One of his many responsibilities was to oversee the education of diocesan seminarians studying in various parts of the country. Beiting was impressed with Bishop Mulloy, "who seemed to know where he was going and determined to get there. He was always very outgoing and had charisma. The bishop also had an Irish temper that would flare up from time to time. However, he was a man totally dedicated to the church, who took great interest in the seminarians, which made sharing the Catholic faith with him a real joy." [15]

One of Bishop Mulloy's first initiatives had a profound affect on Beiting. "He worked hard to change the attitude of clergy who felt that service in Eastern Kentucky was like living in exile until repentance was made. But, the bishop wanted priests to have a great deal of liberty. One of his first actions gave priests, who were serving in the mountain areas, an opportunity to stay or come back to Northern Kentucky," says Beiting. [16]

To meet the need for more priests, Bishop Mulloy brought into the mountain region of the Covington Diocese religious orders such as the Benedictines, Franciscans, Oblates of Mary Immaculate, the Precious Blood and Trinitarian fathers. He also desired to instill enthusiasm in the seminarians about working in Appalachia. His plan called for a number of them to intern in the mountains during the summer months, and hoped they would come back with a sense of excitement.[17]

In 1946, Bishop Mulloy assigned Beiting and fellow seminarian Tom Brennan as summer interns to assist Father Joseph Wimmers, pastor of St. Michael's Mission Church, at Paintsville, Kentucky. Located in the eastern section of the state, Paintsville served as the home base for their work in a five county area. It was a strange summer: World War II had been over for almost a year, and production in the coal fields decreased severely. Coal was no longer needed to support the war effort. A deep recession, exclusive to the mountain region, led to high unemployment. As a result, an extensive migration of people from Appalachia painted a picture of hopelessness to young Beiting.

> *I knew something of poverty and had grown up poor in the midst of the Great Depression, but what I saw that summer in Eastern Kentucky was something far beyond the normal concept of poverty. The only word to adequately describe it is destitution ...so many of those people simply had no way of surviving.*[18]

Mining was the only source of employment for many mountaineers, and when coal corporations closed down and moved out, the people were left to fend for themselves. Many had to develop their own future, which proved to be difficult since very few were prepared for this task.

As Beiting worked with Father Wimmers and a Passionist priest from Tennessee, Cornelius McGraw, he saw their deep commitment to the faith and the desire to help the poor. Their friendship, support and kindness greatly enriched Beiting's growing feelings of closeness for the Appalachian people. "Experiences were many, and I saw the real meaning of what priesthood entailed in Appalachia. It was exhilarating, a mixture of the religious life and secular world."[19]

During that summer of 1946, the seminarians actively participated in the development of St. Michael's Mission School in Paintsville.[20] Previously, the diocese had bought an old mansion, which had fallen into disrepair, and it became their task to transform it into a school by late August.[21] That same summer, the seminarians taught Bible school. Children came from neighboring counties and boarded at the mansion for a two-week period, as Beiting, Brennan and the Sisters of Divine Providence instructed them.[22]

Beiting and fellow seminarian, assigned interns at St. Michael's Mission Church at Paintsville, Kentucky

Most impressive to Beiting about missionary work in Appalachia was Father Wimmers' persistence and dedication to spread the Word of God to the needy. Street preaching proved to be an effective way to reach the people. Fathers Wimmers and McGraw, with the help of Beiting and Brennan, preached primarily in county seats in front of general stores, post offices, or places where people would congregate.

The mountain folks were generally tolerant, and the missionaries reached many through the common bond of the Bible. However, at times, certain individuals were disrespectful and became hostile, and threw tomatoes or rocks at the priests and seminarians. Once, the clergymen were the target of gunfire. Fortunately, no one was hurt, and this incident did not distract their fortitude and faith, and they continued preaching peace and love.

Beiting first preached on the grounds of St. Casimir Church in Van Lear, a small mining community. St. Casimir, established in 1911, was the first Catholic church in far Eastern Kentucky. The Catholic population in Van Lear consisted mainly of Polish miners who moved to the area during the early part of the 20th century. Just a few miles up the road from Van Lear was Butcher Hollow, which became famous in later years as Loretta Lynn's birthplace.[23] The movie *Coal Miner's Daughter* was partially filmed there. Beiting sometimes wondered if Loretta was one of the children in the audience who came to listen that afternoon he preached. Later, he wrote of his preaching experience. "For me, it was an exciting new adventure. I had never seen this aspect of our faith before and I became impressed by it.[24]

An integral part of the summer experience was Mass. Because of the scarcity of Catholic churches in the mountains, services were offered in a variety of settings. Beiting marveled at how these people may have lacked the physical facilities to gather for God's Word and Sacraments, but the importance of Mass was absolute, with value and meaning, regardless of where they worshipped. He remembers Floyd County, where Mass took place in one family's apartment in Martin above a grocery store, a parishioner's garage in Prestonsburg, and at a community church in Wheelwright. Beiting recalls the few wooden churches, the size of small houses, in Wayland, Beauty, West

Liberty, Van Lear, and Paintsville, where people attended Mass regularly. All these places of worship left him with fond memories and a spiritual lift.

Life in Appalachia during the summer of 1946 was not only a period of great challenge for Ralph William Beiting, but also one of inspiration. He had witnessed the vision of Father Wimmers, whose desire was to bring about change and improve the lives of the Appalachian people. At this time, one of the greatest needs in the area was good health care. In the town of Martin, a private hospital had fallen on financial hard times. It appeared that conditions might worsen. The property was for sale and Father Wimmers worried that the hospital might close and leave people without needed health services. He notified the bishop of his concerns. As a result, the hospital was purchased and the Sisters of the Divine Providence agreed to take over the management. This hospital continues to provide help and charity to the people of Eastern Kentucky.[25]

Reflecting upon his summer work, Beiting wrote: "It was at this time that I fell in love with Appalachia and wanted to be involved in something very exciting." This was an awakening that left an indelible impression on him, because he saw poverty and isolationism as he had never seen before. He observed the scarcity of the church and the prejudice at its doorstep. In spite of this, he witnessed the church's reaction of setting up a hospital and school, as well as providing outreach services from the mission parish to people in need. Before leaving Appalachia for his final years at the seminary, he thanked Father Wimmers for allowing him to be a part of this overpowering experience. It would have an everlasting effect on him.[26]

Upon returning to Mount St. Mary seminary, Beiting had an in-depth talk with professor and advisor Father Robert Krumholtz concerning his conviction to do extra tutorial study for future work in Appalachia.

These people were very much attached to the Bible,
they counted on it for almost everything in their life.
And if I was going to be an effective tool in bringing
Catholic teaching to the minds and hearts of these
people, I was going to have to know the Scriptures,
and be able to quote them.[27]

Under the guidance of Krumholtz and other professors, Beiting was provided a comprehensive and balanced learning experience for working in evangelization ministry. "I wanted to be an effective voice similar to that of Father Wimmers and Father McGraw, regarding street preaching," he said.

Ralph William Beiting's two years at Mt. St. Mary's of the West were filled with a rich tradition of caring for others, which brought to light the importance of ecumenism, way before the Ecumenical Council was formed by Pope John XXIII in 1961. This created a strong base for his future work in Appalachia. Beiting recalls a meeting with Father Krumholtz in his last days at Mount St. Mary:

Father Krumholtz took me aside one day. "What do
you plan to do with your faith," he asked.

"I guess I'm going to live it," I answered, hoping that
was the right thing to say.

"Promise me that you'll never look down on some-
one else's faith. Be strong in your own, so you won't
feel the need to belittle the faith of others. Be secure,
so you can work with others and not oppose them,"
he implored.

I can't thank him enough for teaching me that. I think he was a pioneer in ecumenism long before it became a watchword, and his message paid me great dividends when I came to Appalachia, where so many people had different faiths from my own.[28]

For Beiting, the significance of this meeting along with many other experiences, all came together in a unified way. As a result, it gave him a sense of direction and purpose. His future looked promising and he received recognition by others, including the bishop, who knew of this seminarian's accomplishments and potential. Bishop Mulloy had also gained a greater awareness of Beiting's work during the Appalachian summer internship, and felt that further study at Catholic University would blend in with his needs and interests.

When Beiting arrived in Washington, D.C., in August 1947, he stayed at the Sulpician House and trained in the Theological College at the Catholic University of America. His experience with this religious order proved to be of inestimable value. Sulpician priests were recognized worldwide for their seminarian training approach. "It was the beginning of a good relationship with this group of priests, wise in the way they trained seminarians," Beiting said. "I found myself very much involved with them. The Sulpician teachings helped seminarians recognize their power, which raised expectations for a life of richness in serving church and society."[29]

There were many reasons why Beiting considered himself fortunate to attend Catholic University for his last two years of preparation for priesthood. It gave him the opportunity to work with internationally known figures, and provided an off-campus schedule of activities that went beyond traditional ways in servicing the community, along with a continuing process of initiation into the ministry.

One of the most engaging clergy under whom he studied was Father Francis O'Connell, a Redemptorist priest, and a foremost authority on Moral Theology. O'Connell's teachings were a baptism in moral theology for Beiting, reinforcing his Christian faith and a life of fulfillment. To him, Father O'Connell had been the standard of integrity: "As one of the leaders of our church, it filled me with a sense of humility that this man of renown would take the time from his heavy schedule to work with me individually...and provide the courses that I would not otherwise have been able to receive," he recalls.[30]

Beiting's classes at Catholic University were diverse, ranging from one-on-one tutorial sessions to large seminars. Some of his most telling experiences came about through audited courses, which he felt would broaden his knowledge and reasoned judgment. He was eager to absorb intellectual brilliance that emanated from some of the great thinkers. A major figure within that group was one of the most eloquent contributors to preaching, the legendary Fulton J. Sheen, then a monsignor who taught philosophy. Beiting was profoundly moved by Sheen's insight and prophetic nature of things to come.

> *I recall him saying that one of the greatest troubles society would face in the next fifty years is the denial of original sin...people would think that there was no such thing as sin...free to do what he or she thought to be wise and best...there would be no sense of guilt...always pushing for what they want. Monsignor Sheen would live long enough to see his prophecy come about. Nonetheless, it was inspiring to be at the feet of such a man who was a great influence on my life in many ways.[31]*

Sheen struck the right note with Beiting, who also observed the popular orator at St. Matthew Cathedral give instructions before large groups of converts.[32] Monsignor Sheen's training sessions were encouraging to the young seminarian, for this would be an important part of his own work in the ministry. Fulton J. Sheen began to attract nationwide attention for his teaching and lecturing in the 1930s. During that period, he was the first regular speaker of the Catholic Hour on radio, and by the late 1940s had reached four million listeners each week. Later in the 1950s, he began a television program entitled "Life Is Worth Living" that aired to approximately thirty million people. When Ralph William Beiting eventually went to serve in Appalachia, Sheen, now a bishop, was the most popular television personality of the mountain people. For Beiting, this was an advantage: "If I said I was from the same group that Bishop Sheen was a part of, it became a plus for me."[33]

One of the most interesting reflections of Beiting's training was the role of the church in social improvement. Even though two essential points of the Catholic doctrine were social justice and charity, he felt that the church needed to play a more active role. "After all, one of its important teachings is the obligation to apply the gospel to society's poor, oppressed, and powerless."[34] At an early age, Beiting was taught to reach out and help others. As the years progressed, his concern for the less fortunate became stronger. His vision for social improvement in Appalachia was further reinforced by the training at Catholic University, and work activities in Washington, D.C. In turn, this helped him to determine that his future ministry would not only include celebration of the sacraments and preaching of the gospel, but social justice as well.

During his stay in the capitol, a major social issue of concern was racial segregation. Interracial groups and organizations were undertaking projects to improve race relations and end discriminatory policies and practices. Beiting became interested in this work because he felt that segregation was morally wrong and sinful. The frustration of people being held down and unable to feel good about themselves was not new to him. "Kentucky, my home state, was divided racially in those days and I had a deep sense that the church needed to be involved with equality for all people," he remembers.[35]

The intensity of labor movement happenings in Washington, D.C., at this time, along with being in the center of the civil rights beginnings, gave Beiting the opportunity to meet with leaders of various movements. Clarence Mitchell, Labor Secretary for the National Association for the Advancement of Colored People (NAACP) from 1945 to 1950, was one of those leaders who had left a lasting impression on this seminarian. "He was a man of great substance, whose career was outstanding as a spearhead of this reform organization that fought many battles against discrimination. Mr. Mitchell gave me much time to come and visit with him and share some of his insights about the present and future. He was a key to America's awakening," Beiting said. "Later on, he grew to even greater stature and secured his place in the history of civil rights."[36]

Beiting's interest in the labor movement and its changing direction provided him with many opportunities to meet with people from the U.S. Department of Labor, and the AFL-CIO to learn about the struggles of labor. He gained much from the influence of Father George Higgins, a Jesuit priest, and quite an authority on the labor movement. Often, top government and labor officials called upon Higgins for his expertise and knowledge of social reform in the workplace. "To this day, he is still respected for his contributions, and his gift of helping others lives on in those people he has touched," Beiting says.[37]

As part of Beiting's work experience, he had a one-year assignment at Howard University in Washington, D.C., where he conducted studies at the Newman Center. This was a most memorable experience, as he gained great insight into the black culture that was striving for educational excellence and a rightful place in American society. Recognized for his sincerity, the students gained immensely from Beiting's interpretation of social justice and the church. He made them aware that what they were striving for was in complete harmony with the Catholic doctrine. Soon he gained a reputation as a concerned and inspiring teacher. He divided his daily schedule between studies at Catholic University with teaching and coordinating activities at Howard, which started in the morning and ended late at night.[38]

In addition, Beiting taught catechism part-time to Catholics who were studying at the Friends School in D.C., operated by the Quakers. His ability to work among the Quakers with a common goal appealed to them and proved to be valuable. It also provided a touch of the ecumenical spirit of cooperation, as he found Quaker simplicity and goodness heartwarming.[39]

In the spring of 1948, Ralph William Beiting completed his seventh year of preparation for the priesthood at Catholic University. Beiting's pledge to priesthood further came into focus as he moved closer to completing his theology studies. As a subdeacon, he made promises of celibacy, obedience, and commitment to the church. There never was a question of him entering the priesthood. However, there were moments during seminary life when he had to draw strength and clarity of purpose to reaffirm his direction in serving God. Forsaking marriage and family was not an easy decision for him to make, especially since his upbringing was rich in family life and love.

I didn't know how faithful I could be in the exercise of those functions, but I was asked to accept that challenge. The idea of not being married and a father wasn't something to be taken lightly, because I love children. ...I was deeply grateful that there were eleven children in our family...and saw children as a blessing, not a burden...I saw family love and life as something noble, beautiful, and certainly did not willingly throw those values aside. I was asked to sacrifice...to be without a companion and children of my own, and the strength that would come with a family around me. ...It was not something that I enjoyed giving up, and I had envisioned having children like my parents. This was not easy to give up, but was worth the cause that God asked of me...the priesthood was a special calling, and while I didn't deserve it or know how well I could perform, I was willing to give my best effort to bring it about.[40]

On the grounds of the University stood the largest Roman Catholic Church in the U.S.—The National Shrine of the Immaculate Conception, where Beiting completed his final year of training. This Shrine was established by the American bishops who chose Mary as patroness of the United States under her title of the Immaculate Conception. It was here that his ordination as a deacon took place, and where he served the fall of 1948 through the spring of 1949. He was very grateful for the opportunity to start his ministerial work in this church. Later, he said, "It was exhilarating to renew my devotion to the Mother of Jesus at this holy place."[41]

His role as deacon included responsibilities that ranged from assisting priests at Mass, directing liturgical services, and working with the community. The National Shrine, supervised by the American bishops, served a population with a great diversity of backgrounds. People from all walks of life, including government officials and foreign dignitaries, came to worship. In addition, a multitude of visitors showed up daily to view this ecclesiastical wonder. It was inspiring to Beiting to see how the Shrine provided an unparalleled atmosphere and direction for spiritual growth.

At this time, the total inner structure of the church was not completed. However, the people attended service while construction was ongoing. Beiting relates to this experience.

> *I remember when we were asked to serve a special Mass to bless the combined deliberations of Congress and the Supreme Court. Services were held in the basement because only the foundation of the Shrine was completed, but the upper inner structure was not finished. It would take over another decade for this beautiful edifice to be concluded. Yet the experience of being involved on the ground floor was so enlightening and exciting.*[42]

One aspect of Beiting's deaconship included spiritual caregiving to hospital patients in Metropolitan D.C. He was no longer just studying, but exercised ministerial duties for the people. His daily schedule consisted of comforting the sick and dying, administering communion, and providing counseling. These experiences varied since his schedule called for him to visit city hospitals, which accommodated many poor people, and government health facilities, like Walter Reed, whose patients were veterans.[43]

Even as a novice, he brought to the patients and their families a feeling of confidence and spiritual uplift. This came about because of his genuine caring and commitment to listening. Through his reverence for them, Beiting experienced an intense spiritual union with the people. He found joy in discovering that one can make a difference and get results by working effectively with patients to help them access their spirituality. In turn, this gave them ultimate meaning in their lives. Through his counseling, they found faith and prayer, great solace, and the courage to face their medical crisis.

May of 1948 was a period of great anticipation, and Ralph William Beiting's fervor increased as he grew closer to priesthood.[44] Having received a Licentiate Sacred Theology Degree (STL) from Catholic University and ending his work at the National Shrine, he knelt in church for hours at a time, engaged in prayer and contemplation. Beiting's vision of Appalachia and the situation of the poor weighed heavily on his heart. Aware of the type of priest he wanted to become, his indomitable spirit and determination would lead him toward a religious and humanitarian mission. He would focus on working with the total community, doing good deeds for not only Catholics, but for all people, especially the poor.

Finally, the time of ultimate expectation made its appearance, and he bid farewell to Catholic University and the Shrine of Immaculate Conception. As Ralph William Beiting boarded the train at Union Station, he looked back and remembered the historical greatness of Washington, D.C., and his warm feelings for its people. He returned to Covington, Kentucky, and immediately became involved in a week-long retreat and preparation for his ordination.

Young Father Beiting administering blessings

CHAPTER III

THE PRIESTHOOD

Twenty-five year old Ralph William Beiting was ordained to the priesthood at St. Mary's Cathedral in Covington, Kentucky, on Saturday, June 4, 1949. Of the six young men ordained, only Beiting and Vincent F. Schmidt of Bellevue were from the Covington Diocese, while the others came from midwestern and eastern states to serve under Bishop Mulloy's authority. Even though Father Beiting is the only living survivor of that group, he still reflects with affection on this most symbolic event and how their "subsequent friendship and commitment to the priesthood remained constant through the years."[1]

He remembers how the beautiful gothic church was filled to capacity, that people wore their Sunday finery, in a Saturday state of mind. It was a day of rejoicing and happiness as Beiting's proud parents, brothers, sisters, relatives, and friends were among those in attendance. His sister, Dorothy, recalls how the family couldn't contain their enthusiasm. "We were all so proud of him and felt he was going to be an outstanding priest."[2] Another sister, Martha, was so inspired by her oldest brother's commitment to God that she entered a convent in 1954, and dedicated her life as a nun with the Sisters of Notre Dame.

As the ceremony progressed, the imposition of Bishop

Mulloy's hands on each ordinand's head represented the essential rite of ordination. Following this, the ordinands lay prostate on the cathedral marble floor, as attending priests prayed over them and the congregation sang the Litany of Saints. After the prayer of consecration, the newly ordained priests were each vested with stole and chasuble. The bishop anointed their hands with holy oil, and presented them with a chalice and paten containing wine and a host, showing that they had the power to offer Mass. "We promised obedience to the bishop that day and to his successors in office as long as we should live," Beiting remembers. "It was a day that is still very sacred to me...and the memory of it continues cherished in my heart."[3]

After the inspiring celebration, which combined a traditional Catholic Mass and ordination rite, Bishop Mulloy held a reception for the new clergy and their parents in the Chancery. Each new priest, wondering where he would be sent to serve, waited with great anticipation. However, the answer would not come until a week later. This did not dim the happy mood, for it was a time of great fulfillment and Beiting looked forward to celebrating his first Mass on Sunday, June 5, at St. Joseph's Church in Cold Spring.

It was at St. Joseph that Beiting had received all the sacraments except his baptism, served as an altar boy, and attended Mass until entering the seminary. Along the way, he made many friends among the clergy, and now that he was one of them, they wanted to be with him to help celebrate his first Mass.[4] They included Monsignor Leo Streck, former pastor at St. Joseph from 1934 until 1948, Father Lawrence Leinheuser, then pastor of St. Joseph, Reverend Leo Kampsen, who gave the sermon, Reverend Urban A. Horstman, his Newport Catholic High School principal, Father John Hegenauer, the present principal, and his friend Father John Murphy from Catholic Univer-

Newly-ordained Father Beiting prepares to celebrate his first Mass on June 5th at St. Joseph's Church in Cold Spring, Kentucky

sity. Most of the parish crowd had known Ralph William Beiting since he was a child. This momentous occasion culminated the many years of interest in his progression to priesthood. For the Beiting family, it was significant that their oldest son had achieved the ultimate they could ask for—he became a priest.[5]

One week later, the letter from Bishop Mulloy arrived, notifying Father Beiting of his assignment as associate pastor at St. Bernard parish in Dayton, in Northern Kentucky. He would also teach four math classes a day at Newport Catholic High School, direct the debate team, and serve as faculty advisor to the student newspaper. Even though he had anticipated going to Appalachia, Beiting accepted his assignment with humility and a positive attitude. The bishop never told him the reason for his decision. He possibly felt that the young priest should have a smooth transition, getting his feet wet in a parish that consisted of many needy people.

In preparing himself for his new assignments, Beiting immediately met with Father Hubert Schmitz, pastor of St. Bernard Church, and the high school principal, Father John Hegenhauer. "Father Schmitz was an encouraging leader, and a fine and kind man to me as well," Beiting wrote in later years. "The parishioners had been ordinary folks who were poor, and very few possessed any great material means. In spite of their problems of poverty, they were wonderful people who I will always treasure."[6] In his own special way, Beiting would leave parishioners and the community with spiritual and humanitarian gifts for years to come.

Teaching at Newport Catholic was a small token of his appreciation for all he had gained by attending this school. "I could return in some fashion something of the benefits that I had received there," he recalls.[7] However, Beiting's teaching experience was presented with some interesting situations, to say the least. For instance, it was rare for a high school to boast having a priest as a teacher, whose younger brother attended his class. Such was the case with Father Beiting and his brother, Jim, "When I first enrolled in his class, I felt very hesitant. My biggest worry was that he would make me work harder, so others wouldn't think I'd be given favored treatment," Jim Beiting remembers. "But he was fair and compassionate in dealing not only with me, but the other students as well."[8]

Student teachers were also a part of the classroom scene at Newport Catholic. Math majors from Xavier University of Cincinnati did their student teaching in Father Beiting's classes. On one occasion, a young man tried to teach, and Beiting had received instructions to observe him. "He almost went crazy...the students did so many things to test his patience that he finally said to me, "I think I'd rather work in a coal mine than teach." I was a little bit more fortunate, being a little older than he. Also, I was a priest, and that cut some weight with the students."

Certainly, the students at Newport Catholic High were hardly unique in their inclination for testing teachers. This was and still is commonplace, but not deemed acceptable behavior. Father Beiting's students knew where he stood in class, "especially those who couldn't cut algebra and had to take general math." This was the type of class where youngsters needed an extra push and help in the right direction. He was a task master, yet felt that some needed encouragement. Whatever their preoccupations were in class, he immediately established the ground rules.[9]

> *I said to them right off the bat. ...I want you to know one thing, it's up to you as to what happens. ...If you're going to horse around, or act up in class, you're going to stay after school...and don't give me the excuse that you can't stay, because you have a job after school...or your mother is dying...or your father was in an accident...because none of these excuses are going to work. I will stay with you here until five o'clock.*

Father Beiting challenged them, and if they tried to test him, he was true to his word. He expected students to be responsible for their actions, as inner motivation and self-discipline were key goals in his classroom. Beiting felt that the learning environment had to draw on the elements of individual differences, which prepared them to deal with a complex and demanding society. The students understood that he cared for them and wanted each and every one to succeed. Above all, he was their friend and motivator. One of the most rewarding results of Beiting's work occurred when some of these former students served later as volunteers in his Appalachian crusade.

As Father Beiting started his work at St. Bernard parish, he did not come to the people with answers, but a willingness to be a facilitator, developing a genuine Christian community. What impressed him was the cooperative spirit of these people, their response to his style of pastoral work, and the willingness to help and participate. He liked to go out into the community and visit Catholics and non-Catholics. In turn, they were impressed with his honesty and sincerity. Beiting brought comfort to them, cared about their needs and concerns, and became a part of their lives. During a fourteen-month period, he was responsible for over fifty converts to Catholicism.[10]

One of the most enduring legends of Father Beiting's experiences that still persists, is the St. Bernard's parish baseball team. When he arrived that June, the baseball season was half completed and the team had a dismal record, yet he decided to join and played shortstop. Though St. Bernard finished last in the inter-parish league, one would have been hard-pressed to find a greater competitor than Beiting. He just wouldn't give up, even when the season was over, and took it upon himself to rebuild the team. Father Beiting called the players together and announced that they were going to win the championship the next season. They were skeptic, but he presented to them a strategy of how they could achieve this. Working hard by practicing their skills over the winter and recruiting other talented young athletes in the parish became two major objectives. Many young men who did not participate on the team were no longer going to church, but Beiting got them interested in attending Mass. He spent fall and winter persuading these individuals and others to join, assuring them that St. Bernard was going to have the best baseball team in the entire Northern Kentucky area. When spring came, the new and old team members started to practice. They worked hard as a cohesive unit, and Beiting, their leader, played shortstop as well.[11]

That summer the team achieved glory, as it exemplified the spirit, character, and competitiveness of its leader. They had won fifteen games before finally losing. That one loss sobered the team up, and the players rededicated themselves. On the last day of the season, they played the same team that had beaten them, but this time St. Bernard won by a lopsided score. With that victory, St. Bernard's baseball team went on to the regional playoffs, representing the Holy Name city inter-parish league, winning the division championship and finishing with the best record in Northern Kentucky.

At the end of Father Beiting's first year of teaching, the Newport Catholic principal called him into his office. Father Hegenauer was surprised that this priest, liked by the students, faculty and administration during his short term there, was not reassigned for the coming school year. He was disappointed and wondered what the Diocesan office had in mind. Beiting answered that he had not received any information about his future situation. A few days later, Father Schmitz, who also had grown to admire his young assistant's work, called Beiting into his office and asked him, "What is this? I get a letter from the bishop saying you are no longer staying here." Befuddled, Beiting replied that he enjoyed his work as both assistant pastor and teacher, and had no idea what the bishop had planned for him.[12]

Bishop Mulloy eventually showed up at St. Bernard Church on Labor Day to celebrate Mass. Later that morning, he asked Father Beiting to meet with him in the church office. Puzzled by the cumulative effect of the circumstances, the young priest tried to make himself comfortable in Mulloy's presence. The bishop explained that he had gone over his record, which filled Beiting with a sense of trepidation.

> *How much of the record did he know, I asked myself? If he was all-knowing, I could be in real trouble. The bishop went on, 'I have been giving considerable thought to opening a new mission territory in our Appalachian area. I need to select a priest to act as a pastor for four counties in the area, and I think you would be a good selection.' I couldn't believe what I was hearing. Surely this was some ecclesiastical test to determine the degree of a person's humility! Or maybe what they taught us in the seminary was true, that the inspiration of the Holy Spirit was the motivating force behind this decision. Fortified by this thought, I asked the bishop the location of the church. He said, 'there is no church.' I told myself I couldn't have everything in Appalachia the first time around, and went on to serious matters. 'Where is the rectory?' was my next question. 'There's no rectory either,' the bishop told me. Right then and there I had a serious reservation about the Holy Spirit being involved in this affair at all.[13]*

Ordained just over a year, Beiting's designated assignment by the bishop appeared not in the normal order of things. However, he knew that the Covington Diocese urgently needed priests to carry on the work of the church in Appalachia. To become a pastor generally required a greater number of years of service. Yet, Bishop Mulloy felt very strongly about developing this new parish because he believed that the church was the most important tool to help transform the people of Appalachia, both spiritually and socially.

The bishop selected Berea, Kentucky, as the center for Beiting's work, who later found out about the rationale for this decision. During those years, Berea College students were not allowed to leave the community and there was no church in town available for Catholics to attend Mass. One student, a friend of former U.S. Representative Clare Booth Luce, contacted her to see if it was possible to build a Catholic chapel in Berea.[14] Mrs. Luce, wife of the publisher of *Time* and *Look* magazines, and a convert to Catholicism, responded that she would be glad to help finance the building of a new chapel. As a result, the Covington Diocese invited her to give a series of speeches in January of 1950. Contributions from these events were set aside for the development of a religious facility. The diocese bought property with a house, and the Congregation of the Holy Ghost Fathers agreed to send a priest to establish a chapel as well as provide services to the surrounding area.

That spring, Bishop Mulloy traveled to Rome, Italy, and met with the head of the Holy Ghost Fathers, who told him that after looking into the situation, they were unable to fulfill the commitment. Meanwhile, Bishop Mulloy had assured the former congresswoman that dedication of the chapel was planned for the fall of 1950, naming it St. Clare in honor of Mrs. Luce.[15]

After the Holy Ghost Fathers withdrew, the bishop continued to look for someone in his own diocese with the pastoral vision and leadership who would develop a mission unique to Appalachia's needs. To Father Beiting, it may have appeared that his selection by Bishop Mulloy was from out of the blue.

*Apparently the bishop felt that he needed someone
young, who didn't know what he was up against,
and would be willing to go to the mountains. I fitted
that category, I suspect, rather well.*[16]

However, Mulloy's reason for selecting Ralph William
Beiting came from the bishop's conviction that strong leadership was needed to make the Church present and active in
Appalachia. Bishop Mulloy knew that Father Beiting had the
potential to effectively provide evangelization to this area of
poverty and isolation. He admired his contribution as a seminarian, particularly during the summer work in Appalachia and
the two years at Washington, D.C.[17] The bishop also witnessed
the effectiveness of Beiting's ministry at St. Bernard as well as
Newport Catholic, and felt confident that he would do a fine
job.

It took Father Beiting a few days to adjust to the idea, but he
soon realized that his first appointment as pastor would be
challenging and exciting, like "St. Peter in the building of a new
mission."

CHAPTER IV

THE EARLY YEARS IN APPALACHIA

When Father Ralph William Beiting arrived in Appalachia in the fall of 1950, coal mining, the single major industry, had experienced a great decline. This led to unbelievable heights of unemployment and a mass exodus of people from the mountain country. The few Catholics who lived in eastern Kentucky before 1950, dwindled even further as many coal towns ceased to exist. Right from the beginning, Father Beiting became aware of the people's religious needs and their long-standing problem of poverty. In spite of the situation, his assignment was to start a parish that covered four counties—Garrard, Jackson, southern Madison and Rockcastle. Organizing and developing the Catholic Church in such a widespread area compounded the many problems Beiting had to face. This challenge was further perpetuated by his desire to help the impoverished in every way regardless of their religious background, which would become the trademark of his work.

October 7, 1950, was an overcast Appalachian day, when Father Beiting drove into Berea on U.S. 25, a two-lane road that also served as main street for this small college town. He turned onto a bumpy gravel driveway marked with potholes, and stopped his car to peer across five-foot high weeds at an old house with eaves, soffits, and shutters hanging in disarray. Stunned by what he saw, Beiting slowly walked to the two-story house that would serve as St. Clare's chapel and living quarters. The porch had rotted and was unsafe—every step on its decaying planks threatened to create a hole. When Beiting walked lightly across the perilous porch and into the house, he noticed that the entire first floor sagged precariously. The previous owners had dug a room under the house for a coal-heated furnace several years before. "They miscalculated the dimensions of the furnace," he recalls. "And when the time came to install it, extra space was made by cutting the beam that supported the floor joists." The consequences created a dangerous situation. Apprehension grew within him as he walked with delicate balance around the house, not wanting to add extra weight to the sagging floor.[1]

It had been unseasonably cold throughout Appalachia, and without heat the temperature in the house seemed no different than outside. After starting a fire in the furnace, Father Beiting soon found that it had worn out its usefulness and the house was barely warmer than before. His assignment to transform this place into a chapel was not encouraging because of limited financial resources. He had less than one hundred dollars in his pocket, and his salary as a priest was forty-one dollars a month, which just about covered personal needs and the use of his car. The diocesan office told him that contributions from the church collections were to furnish the house, provide for food, and all the other things. Since there were only nine Catholics in the Berea area, and three were children, he anticipated very little from the collections.[2]

The circumstances and the quiet that surrounded him in this rundown house brought on a feeling of loneliness. Beiting was faced with a dilemma, and there were no relatives to lean on. He had not met his neighbors, nor was there a welcoming committee or friends he could turn to. For a moment, anxiety took hold of him and he began to raise questions in his mind.

What have I gotten myself into. ...Should I turn back from this foolish pilgrimage. ...Should I get into my car and go back up north? In just a few hours I could be back home with my family. I thought, I am only twenty-six years old, and ordained just a year ago. ...Shouldn't a more experienced man take up this enormous challenge?[3]

Father Beiting contemplated the profound emptiness within himself and went upstairs to his living quarters, which consisted of a bed and chair. He opened an old suitcase, took out a crucifix, that was given to him as a religion award in high school, and hung it on the wall. Looking at the man on the cross brought a sense of closeness. Until that moment, the crucifix had primarily been a reminder of his high school accomplishment. Gradually, he stopped thinking about the engraving with his name on it and began to see Christ on the cross. He started to pray for courage and asked God for guidance.

There was no miraculous answer. Beiting did not see the cross move, or Jesus smile at him. However, God's words from the Bible came to his mind:[4]

Come follow me, ...I will never leave you an orphan. ...Fear not you of little faith...Did you not know I was with you?...With me you can do all things...It is only when you are without me that you can do nothing.

These messages of God's undying love had propelled this

young priest to overcome his weariness, and he remembered Apostle Peter's words to the early persecuted Christians: "Cast all your cares on Him for He loves you." The realization came to him that he had to have a more stout and resolute heart to face the challenge ahead. With his love for God serving as the foundation and by following Jesus' path, Father Beiting recognized that there was a source of strength beyond himself.

That night he could not sleep, because too many things were on his mind. The next morning he got up blurry eyed, but with great expectation, ready to undertake the task of planning to redesign the house into a chapel. Father Beiting may not have had the financial or material resources, but his family's willingness to assist him provided the needed inspiration. His parents, brothers and sisters, along with their spouses, would come to Berea on weekends and help him renovate the house.

With Mr. and Mrs. Beiting running herd on the family, they reconstructed the first floor into a beautiful chapel, and refurbished the upstairs living quarters. They often brought their friends and other people that wanted to help. Thus, the first volunteers were his parents, brothers, sisters and in-laws, who became the most important resource in his pilgrimage. Years later, his brother, Don Beiting, told of the family's closeness and commitment. "I remember us going down to Berea in those early days, sometimes spending two weeks at a time, helping Father Bill (affectionately called by family members). We had experienced great excitement and sensed that he was going to do something significant for the people of Appalachia. Our family was practicing the faith by working together with my brother to make an impact."[5]

As soon as Father Beiting arrived in Berea, prejudice and bigotry were directed toward him and the Catholic Church by a next door neighbor. "This individual had decided he didn't want the place of worship next to his home, and started a petition drive to have the church thrown out of town," Beiting recalls. Rumors were that the man complained, "Berea used to be a nice town, but then we allowed a pool hall to open and now a Catholic Church."[6]

Beiting tried to talk with his neighbor to see if they could develop some kind of understanding. The man insisted that the Catholic Church was not wanted in his town, and they would never be friends. There were many people who did not agree with the petition and it failed, but the man made it known that his feelings hadn't changed. This type of action was the first of many negative experiences that Beiting would encounter.

Over time, the neighbor became more civil, and a few years later he sold his house to St. Clare Church for use as a rectory and volunteer dormitory. One could surmise that he may have wanted to get away from Catholics, but there was a surprising side to this story. Twenty years later, Father Beiting was meeting with community leaders in Berea about a new project he wanted to start, when certain individuals voiced their objections to the proposal. His ex-neighbor stood up and, to the amazement of everyone, said, "You all know I was against Father when he came here, but he's done so much good, and made many people think how they can help others. I've come to believe he's the only minister in town who's worth a damn. I just want him to know that I appreciate what he has done."[7]

Beiting was shocked and surprised that the man called him "Father." "This title is such a symbol of Catholicism that I never anticipated him referring to me that way," he said. Furthermore, the former neighbor had exhibited respect and recognition for this priest, who was moved by the transformation.

I don't think I'll ever get an award or accolade as

*fulfilling or unexpected as that one. And I truly be-
lieve God must have played a role in my neighbor's
change of heart about me.*[8]

As reconstruction of the house in Berea got underway, an emergency situation occurred in a neighboring parish, and Bishop Mulloy assigned Beiting additional duties. He was asked to temporarily assist Monsignor Oscar Poole, pastor of St. Marks, who served the town of Richmond and surrounding counties. This meant that the chapel opening in Berea would be postponed until a later date. Regardless of his many assignments, Beiting carried on with intensity and focus.

Whenever possible, he worked weekdays in Berea, transforming the house into a chapel and attended to other pastoral duties. He also traveled to Garrard, Jackson and Rockcastle counties for spiritual meetings with individuals and groups, and established the direction he would take in the future.

Besides assisting Monsignor Poole at St. Marks Church on certain weeknights and Saturdays, Beiting developed the Newman Club for Catholic students at Eastern State Teachers College in Richmond. Sunday mornings he held early Mass at a chapel in Ravenna, then went on to conduct a late service at St. Theresa's mission in Heidelberg.

After finishing Mass at St. Theresa, he elected to spend Sunday afternoons in Lee County evangelizing. Beiting's strong belief that evangelization should be a major part of his work was put to the test immediately. At first, he took his message to the backwoods areas where he encountered hostility. However, he then met Mrs. Rusha Howell who invited him to preach at a country store she and her husband operated in Yellow Rock, a small community on the Kentucky River, downstream from Heidelberg.

People enjoyed coming into the Howell's store to hear Beiting talk about Christ and the Church. "In those days, no one had TV, and radio reception was very limited, so anyone who was alive and able to hear came and listened," he remembers. "Word spread throughout the area, and with each meeting, the attendance grew. We had lively discussions and there was a sense of great joy and appreciation to be able to speak to these folks."[9]

Meanwhile, a most important event of Beiting's early days in Berea—and one that became crucial to his ministry pertained to "helping weary pilgrims along the way."[10] The house-chapel was located on Chestnut Street, about a mile from an area where numerous poor black and white families lived. They often walked into the center of town, and stopped to chat with him as he repaired and painted the outside of his house. Soon, they became friends and invited him to their homes. Beiting was shocked by the unbelievable living conditions he witnessed. In many of the shacks clear plastic was used for windows, and newspapers covered bare walls. There was hardly any furniture in the dwellings. The people lived without electricity, and at night candles were used to light the rooms. Most houses had no running water or an indoor bathroom. On top of this, mothers were distressed that they did not have enough food and clothing for their children. Beiting reached out by bringing these necessities to them. On one cold, wintry day, as he delivered goods to a family in need, Beiting encountered a heart-wrenching experience.

> *I couldn't help but notice that one room was missing many of its floorboards. ..."What happened in there," I asked. The father of the family told me, "Well, it's been awfully cold, and we didn't have no money*

for wood or coal, so we pulled up some of them boards and used 'em for firewood."[11]

Not only were people starving, living in squalor and hazardous substandard dwellings, other conditions also affected their very existence. Unemployment shattered family situations, people were without any form of medical help, and illiteracy deterred the growth or improvement of a person's life. Good education was lacking and the needs of the handicapped and elderly were ignored. Beiting saw too many people living a life of abandonment, dejection, and deprivation and realized he was faced with a missionary challenge of great magnitude. Yet, this did not dissuade him. He was more determined than ever to help the poor. Soon, others in need came to his door asking for help, and he worked tirelessly to care for them, regardless of their religious belief. Periodically, he drove home to Northern Kentucky and collected money, food, clothing, furniture, and other essentials donated by his family and friends and returned to Berea delivering these gifts to the needy. It was a time when government gave little attention to the poor, when Father Beiting arrived in Appalachia. Very few people throughout the nation showed concern for Appalachia's plight. This hurt Beiting, and he would later say, "Nowhere else in America do people live under such deplorable conditions."[12]

In May of 1951, Beiting's temporary assignment at St. Mark's Parish came to an end, and he began to work full-time in Berea. In August 1951, Bishop Mulloy dedicated St. Clare's Chapel in honor of former Congresswoman Luce for her many contributions to humanity.[13]

As the regular schedule of services got underway, not all was going well with attendance. On Sundays at Mass, Father Beiting looked at a congregation of a handful of people. During the rest of the week, he usually said Mass completely alone, which brought on a feeling of loneliness. While going through the service, his voice would echo back to him as if in mockery.

> *I never felt so foolish or lonely. I often wondered why I didn't just give up . ...I felt as the Israelites must have, wandering in the desert. I prayed that my exile wouldn't be as long. I began to question my calling . ...Maybe I misheard God's voice. Could he really have meant to send me to this place to be so alone and so useless?*[14]

Within a month after the first Mass was held in Berea, Beiting received a phone call from Mrs. Lila Murphy of Brodhead, whose dying husband needed a priest.[15] Mr. and Mrs. Murphy had moved to Brodhead twenty years earlier where they operated a restaurant. At that time, the nearest Catholic Church was forty miles away, which made it difficult for Mr. Murphy to attend mass. Due to his illness, he wanted to make a confession and rejoin the Catholic Church. Father Beiting drove to Brodhead to administer the last rites, and shortly thereafter, Mr. Murphy passed away. After the funeral Mass was held at St. Clare's Chapel, the 78 year-old Mrs. Murphy expressed her desire to know more about the Catholic Church. Father Beiting visited her a number of times, since she was interested in joining, and answered many questions, before her commitment to be baptized was made. "She was the sharpest old lady I've ever met, and the discussions were intellectually stimulating," he recalls.

Later on, when Mrs. Murphy found out that Father Beiting was without domestic help, she insisted on "rescuing this poor young priest from those duties," and became his housekeeper.

"She proved to be a diligent worker, had a tremendous personality and exerted a strong influence on everyone who came in contact with her," he says. Mrs. Murphy lived to the age of 96, and was Father Beiting's first convert in Appalachia and a staunch supporter of the Catholic faith.

In the fall of 1951, the St. Clare congregation grew by including students from Berea College, as Father Beiting energetically reached out to the total community despite deeply rooted prejudice. By effectively projecting Catholicism intellectually and spiritually, Beiting gave the students a sense of identity and leadership. This brought him to the attention of other students, and he became a strong force in bridging the gap between different religious groups on campus. He even impressed certain professors who invited him to talk at the college about the Catholic Church, including its stand on social justice.[16]

One of Beiting's most memorable experiences in Berea came at Christmas time.[17] For many residents of Appalachia, the spirit of Christmas was lacking and obscured by the reality of the emptiness in their hearts. Also, less than twenty percent of the population belonged to organized religion and Beiting wanted to send the people a message. One way he did this was to display a large replica of the stable of Bethlehem with figures commemorating the birth of Christ. An artist from Northern Kentucky made and painted life-size figures of Jesus, Mary, Joseph, the shepherds, wise men and animals. Beiting's father and his brothers arrived in Berea two weeks before Christmas, assembled the stable, and set up the Nativity scene. It took a full day to put together this elaborate display. Christmas trees were placed, and lights covered the entire yard, illuminating the stable as well as the surrounding grounds. When Father Beiting turned the lights on for the Christmas season, people came from all over, causing traffic jams on Chestnut Street (U.S. Route 25), as they stopped to view the display. Each year thereafter, people continued to come during the holiday season to admire the display and talk with Father Beiting as he stood outside every evening discussing the importance of Christ's birth. As time moved on, many of these individuals came to know this priest, and supported his cause, for the good he was doing far outweighed the prejudice that was aimed toward him. A most dramatic example of this transformation was that some people who had lost their faith or were non-adherents to any organized religion attended Mass at St. Clare Chapel.

While he was devoting himself to expanding the chapel in Berea, Beiting also gave attention to starting a mission church in Lancaster, the county seat of Garrard, where the majority of Catholics lived. The first meetings were very fruitful and he was convinced that the people wanted a place of worship.[18] Their community had been without a Catholic church for many years. Originally, a priest who had several other missions to care for, came every so often to say Mass at the local courthouse or a private home. As a result, the lack of a Catholic church building in the county led people to lose their faith or join a different religious group. Some even moved to another area where services were available.

In the weeks that followed these meetings, Father Beiting, Isidore Feldman, a local businessman and member of the congregation, along with realtor Cliff Ledford, looked for property to accommodate a chapel. It took longer than anticipated because of the prejudice against everything that was Catholic. People refused to sell their property to Beiting. Finally, in the spring of 1951, he found land with a home that could be converted into a chapel. It was an ideal location on Lexington Street (U.S. Route 27) which ran through the center of Lancaster.

As Beiting, Feldman, and Ledford surveyed the property, a neighbor who was standing nearby called the realtor over to talk to him. Beiting saw Cliff Ledford shake his head, and eventually they parted. When Ledford came back to Beiting and Feldman, he did not mention the discussion. A few months later, he told them what the neighbor had said to him.

Whatever they offer you for that property, I'll give a thousand dollars more, if you don't allow those Catholics into town. However, Ledford responded, "I have given them my word and I will not go back on it."[19]

Because of Cliff Ledford's honesty, Beiting was able to acquire the property for the diocese, along with a house next door. However, opposition continued toward Father Beiting's endeavors. On the other hand, he was met with kindness by such people as County Judge Forrest Calico, John Lynch and his uncles, and the Feldman family who became his lifelong friends.[20]

With the diocese's acquisition of the Lancaster property in May 1951, Beiting again sent out a call to his parents, brothers and sisters, their spouses and friends. They came on weekends to help him convert the house into a chapel, since the dedication was expected to take place in late September 1951. During that summer, some of his former Newport Catholic High School students volunteered to repair and paint the chapel inside and out, and helped with other chores. "Working as volunteers gave them a sense of participation in helping others, as well as spiritual inspiration by assisting in the creation of a house of worship," Beiting said.[21]

Approximately a week before the dedication of St. William

Chapel in Lancaster, Beiting received a phone call from his mother, informing him that his great-aunt Agnes Schafer had died. Aunt Agnes was a very special person whom he loved dearly, and he accepted his mother's request to conduct the funeral Mass at Newport the following morning. Working very hard and late that evening to put final touches on the chapel, he left around eleven p.m. for his parents' home. When Beiting reached the outskirts of Alexandria in Northern Kentucky, he fell asleep behind the wheel, and the car careened off the road, crashing into a deep ditch. He suffered serious internal and head injuries, and spent ten days in a hospital recovering from the accident. Father Beiting was unable to attend his Aunt Agnes' funeral, and the dedication of St. William Chapel was postponed until after his release from the hospital. The dedication finally took place on Sunday, October 28, 1951.[22]

Returning to his duties, Beiting divided the weekday and Sunday schedules equally between Berea and Lancaster. On Saturdays, he traveled to Rockcastle and Jackson counties to celebrate Mass at the homes of families. The mission churches and home evangelization were exemplary of a Christian community, where the people responded to his style of pastoral guidance and supported him through difficult times. Their perspective about Father Beiting's humanistic outlook was evident by his kindness and charity for the total community which became an asset of his leadership role.

With Beiting's base of operation expanding, he encountered added challenges. The more people he helped, the greater the needs became. This called for weekly trips to Northern Kentucky, but his car was not large enough to accommodate the donated goods for delivery to the poor of the area he served. On one of his visits to the chancery, Beiting was asked by Bishop Mulloy how things were going. He replied that it was difficult to transport the needed goods, because of limited car space. A month later the bishop surprised him with a station wagon, and Beiting vividly recalls that happy incident.

> *The bishop felt that maybe this would be something that could help me in doing the things that had to be done . ...I was so grateful because it had not only been the gift of the station wagon that was important, but the fact that he thought about it, and didn't have to be asked...he was out there scouting around, finding people who would help him pay for it...and made it available for me to carry on the work of the church.*[23]

Father Beiting operated the parish and everything else facing financial uncertainty. He only received $1,000 a year from the Diocesan mission fund, and since his parishioners were few, the Sunday collections could not be relied upon for support. Yet, he accepted every discomfort without a complaint, and forged ahead to find ways to overcome the lack of financial resources.[24]

On one occasion, Beiting gained insight on a unique approach to raise money. He was visiting Monsignor John O'Brien, the pastor of St. Mildred Catholic Church in Somerset, Kentucky. Impressed with the facilities, he asked the monsignor how the money was raised to build the church, rectory, and school. O'Brien answered, "I did it through the telephone book." He had gathered telephone books from major cities, and using names he thought might belong to Catholic people, sent them letters asking for donations. This gave Beiting some similar ideas on how to pursue his own fund raising.

It certainly worked for Monsignor O'Brien, maybe it will work for me. ...I had known through my studies that of the fifty largest cities in the United States, the biggest single religion in any of them was Catholicism, certainly in New York, Chicago, Philadelphia, Boston and Baltimore. ...So I gathered up books from these cities, went through them, targeting names I thought would be Catholic. They were primarily Italian, Irish, German, Polish.[25]

With the help of a friend, Beiting designed an appeal letter called the "Mountain News." He sent out the letters, informing people of what he was trying to accomplish in the area, and asked them for their prayers, as well as in-kind gifts and financial help. The responses were favorable, and with each succeeding letter, contributions increased, which enabled him to expand the church and provide more services for the poor. Through the years, he followed this practice of direct mail and included other fund raising initiatives, such as speaking engagements, visits with individuals, groups and organizations.

By this time, Beiting faced even more demands. At Berea, folks continued to come to his door at the chapel's location on the main highway. "It was amazing to find out how great their needs were," he recalls. "Whenever I visited with these families, often the conditions were far worse than they had indicated. It was a great revelation." In being able to reach these people, he found that his own upbringing enabled him to focus on their problems. He knew that the culture of the mountaineers was based on simple wants and needs, and a moral structure that embodied its closeness. He saw too many families without an income and unable to put food on the table. Since many were existing from day to day, Father Beiting's gifts of food and goods gave them hope. He also helped in other ways, by paying their electric bills, providing financial assistance for medical and other emergency relief situations. For those people who were too embarrassed to accept a handout, Beiting attached clothes on ropes which were strung between trees in front of each chapel rectory on given days. Large signs would read, "Free Clothes."

Continuing to feel that he was not doing enough, Father Beiting expanded the effort and created rummage stores first in Berea, then Lancaster, followed by Rockcastle and Jackson counties. Often, he didn't even have to ask for help—people offered on their own. Typical of such eagerness was a gentleman from Berea, Bill Watson, Sr. In Beiting's book, *Pilgrimage of a Country Preacher*, he gives an account of Watson's graciousness.

> *He was a salesman for a wholesale grocery company and traveled throughout the mountain area. He said, 'Father, whatever you need and I have, it's yours. I have a pickup, and if you need to haul things, you let me know.' I took him up on that offer many times. He was always ready to drop whatever he had been doing and came to my aid with dignity and generosity.*[26]

Father Beiting's first approach of distributing goods in the stores was to give them away. However, he discovered that certain individuals abused his generosity, and came very early on those days when new goods were available, and took the best. Before long, they set up their own little stores and sold the same items, making a profit for themselves. Another discouraging situation presented itself when some people who were without washing machines or running water, didn't bother to wash their dirty clothes. It was easier to throw them away and ask for more clothes at the rummage store.[27]

Beiting knew that safeguards had to be implemented in order for the truly impoverished to benefit from this service. He asked that people pay a small fee for goods, which partially contributed to the upkeep of the rummage stores. However, no one was turned away, if the contribution could not be made.

In those early years, it often was difficult for Beiting to look at his own long-range goals, while continually being faced with a multitude of people whose needs were varied. Yet, he believed that programs for children would serve as a strong foundation for developing other initiatives. He started a Bible school to make an impact on these children. "There was such a need for having a strong religious foundation in their lives," he said. "I knew that parents would make a valuable investment in their children's future by having them involved."[28] The success of this program led Father Beiting to expand it to a two-week overnight summer camp the following year in Lancaster, where children were housed. Bible camp eventually became an annual event and the foundation for many religious education programs.

During the development of St. William Chapel in Lancaster, it was Beiting's wish to start a school.[29] He informed Bishop Mulloy of his desire for Catholics and non-Catholics alike to enjoy a Christian education. As a product of Catholic schools himself, Beiting was aware of their significant impact. Mulloy was very supportive and eager to spread Catholic education throughout Appalachia as a way to preserve the faith of people. Encouraged by the bishop's response, Beiting made plans to renovate a two-story house of an early settler, which was located next to the chapel. With the help of his family and friends, the first floor was changed into classrooms, while the rooms upstairs were converted into living quarters for teachers.

St. William School opened in September of 1952 with an enrollment of thirteen students, and the Sisters of Notre Dame from Covington, Kentucky, sent three nuns to help get it started. Sisters Josine, Celsa, and Mary Cabrini were assigned to teach children from kindergarten through eighth grade.[30]

Because of Beiting's increased activities, it was necessary for him to move from Berea to Lancaster. He converted a small sewing room in the back of the chapel's first floor into his bedroom. Unable to afford hiring a bus driver to transport children to and from school, Beiting assumed that role. In addition, he offered daily Mass in Berea and Lancaster, and spent the rest of each day ready to service every human need of his parishioners and the community.[31]

Beiting's biggest challenge was getting people to overcome their deep-rooted suspicion and superstition toward the Catholic church. By showing his sincerity to help improve their conditions and provide opportunities for hope, he changed certain people's attitude.

Whatever information Bishop Mulloy received about missionary work in the mountains, it focused strongly on Beiting's effectiveness to involve people toward positive action. The bishop also knew of the need for more religious help in Eastern Kentucky, and reversed his decision of the late 1940s, when he disbanded the seminarian summer Appalachian internship. By supporting Beiting's work and his request for interns during the summer months, Bishop Mulloy made a decision that would be rewarding for years to come.

In 1954, seminarians John Rolf, Herman Kamlage, and Laurence Robotnik were sent to Appalachia as interns to serve with Beiting.[32] Starting with these three, a procession of other seminarians followed over the next twenty-plus summers to gain first hand knowledge of Father Beiting's work. Instead of the typical parish situation that many of these young men might come across later as priests, they served with a missionary who was building a bridge of hope for people deprived of so many things in life, including religion. The seminarians observed that spiritual and humanitarian services were complimentary concerns, as the gospel and people of poverty became a necessary link in Beiting's work.[33]

One of Father Beiting's greatest efforts to reach the people was evangelizing through street preaching every summer.[34] Starting on his own in 1951 and expanding in 1954 with the help of seminarians, Beiting carried out the task of preaching in desolated backcountry areas, and eventually throughout all of Eastern Kentucky. His own experience as an intern with Fathers Wimmers and McGraw at Paintsville was of such value that he felt the desire to herald the gospel in this special way to the people of Appalachia. In turn, he wanted the seminarians to experience this aspect of evangelization and understand its importance in missionary work.

Father Beiting and his summer interns traveled extensively, making one-hour outdoor presentations in eight different communities every day. This grueling schedule started early in the morning and lasted late into the night. As the program grew, Beiting and the seminarians "were joined by a group of other priests, nuns, lay people, and Protestant ministers—anyone I could con," he recalls with pride and humor. "It was a way in which we could make our presence known and what the church was all about."[35] With the aid of these helpers who freely gave their support, Beiting wanted people to know that whatever their needs, he and the others were there to help. He continued to return to give them food, goods, and other necessities, as well as spiritual guidance.

The seminarians saw Beiting accept many overwhelming challenges, and witnessed his efforts to eliminate Appalachia's poverty through persistent action. He understood the expansive problems of the poor, and how difficult it was for them to grow socially, economically, physically, and spiritually. Poverty was so intractable that it brought a feeling of resignation and lack of self-esteem, which led to a fatalistic attitude for those people who were painfully in need. For many seminarians, the impact of Father Beiting's work lay mainly in his persevering style of moral support to the people, again knowing that any type of change would take a great amount of time and patience.

Today, Father John Rolf who served those first two summers as a seminarian, remembers specifically Beiting's patience in trying to bring spiritual enlightenment to the people: "There were very few converts in those days, and it amazed me how Father Beiting could persevere and push on. However, he believed that through hard work, and God's blessing, things would come about."[36]

When Father Beiting first came to Appalachia, he knew he had to work extremely hard and practice the principles of deferred gratification. Trust was very important to the Appalachian people, and the mention of Catholicism had a bad connotation for many of them. In order for him to help the poor who he saw hurt time after time, he was willing to take small steps to make these people feel comfortable with the Catholic Church. In his book, *Appalachia...A Special Place...A Bridge of Hope*, Beiting gave insight of his feelings and why the conditions existed. [37]

Although I was raised a Catholic and love the Catholic faith so much that I have dedicated my life to it as a Catholic priest, I know Baptists and Lutherans worship the same Risen Lord and the same God. I know that Jesus said, 'Whoever is not against us is with us.' I know that only when all of God's people join together can we end the poverty and despair of His people.

I have always looked for ways that I can meet other people of God halfway and even go that extra step. Yet, people who have been isolated as long as the people of Appalachia are usually mistrustful of outsiders. ...Generations of mistrust had instilled in the people a fear of Catholics, and as a priest I was the embodiment of that fear. Most people had never even met a Catholic, yet they were convinced we were evil and murderous and blasphemous.

I don't fault the Appalachian people for these prejudices. These fears came to America from medieval Europe and thrived in the isolation of Appalachia. Through the centuries, Catholics have been guilty of the same kind of prejudices towards Protestants and other believers. That's why we need to build bridges between all of God's people.

Although most of Beiting's spiritual work took place in Lancaster and Berea, where the majority of his parishioners lived, this did not deter him from providing service to people of Jackson and Rockcastle. As a missionary, he felt obliged to spread the word of God the best possible way he could. Beginning in 1951, home visitation was a major part of his work in these counties, for he would not build mission chapels there until the early 1960s. Very few Catholics lived in Jackson and

Rockcastle, and their hardships increased Beiting's sense of destiny and mission. They may not have been able to travel to church, but belief in God was the underlying factor of their daily existence. Thus, they worshipped at home with the Bible as their foundation. Beiting admired the determination of these folks because, in spite of their hardships, they sustained themselves by living in harmony with the environment. They were of strong character, and isolation made them depend on God and family.

Of the four counties in Father Beiting's parish, Jackson was the most mountainous and poorest. Catholics were few and far between so when he was able to locate a family, they rejoiced and were appreciative. Jackson was very remote and removed from the outside world. One of his first contacts in this county was Tom Conlin, who lived on Horse Lick—nothing more than a creek and a few houses in the wilderness.[38] On his initial visit, Father Beiting spent a frustrating amount of time trying to find him. He traveled endlessly on a narrow, winding and dangerous road that started out as black top, became gravel and finally ended in a creek. The road, established as a footpath a century earlier, led over and around mountains to nowhere. As he viewed his unpredictable situation with consternation, a man came walking along the creek toward the car. Beiting called out to him, asking if he knew of Tom Conlin. Looking at the car, the man noticed a rosary hanging from the rearview mirror. He proudly said, "Yes, I am Conlin, and I'm Catholic." Without a break of breath in his voice, Mr. Conlin made Beiting aware that he had taken a fancy to the rosary, and asked if he could have it. Conlin then told that he had not seen a priest in twenty years. He came to Appalachia from Ohio during the Depression, worked with the government-sponsored Civilian Conservation Corps program, married a local woman, and settled there.

In those days, professing that he was a Catholic had been difficult for Tom Conlin or anyone else of the same persuasion. If individuals did not have the same religious conviction as the majority of people in this area, they were discriminated against. However, Conlin proved to be of great support to Beiting's work with the folks of Jackson County. When Father Beiting built the mission church in McKee years later, Conlin moved there and lived in the rectory until he died. The rosary that Beiting gave him on that first meeting was placed in Conlin's hands before his burial. Finding this man at Horse Lick was "not by accident, but the providence of God," Beiting later said.

Father Beiting's mission work in each county had its own unique characteristic. For example, in Rockcastle, his efforts brought great gratification even though there were only a few Catholic families living in the county. One of them was the Tom and Dorothy Mullins family and their three sons from Mt. Vernon.[39] Mr. Mullins was the nephew of John Lair, a famous mountain man, who promoted entertainment in Kentucky. He founded Renfro Valley, a country music mecca second only to Nashville. The Mullins family looked forward to Beiting's visits and he in turn, enjoyed their company as well. Tom Mullins knew that chairs and other items were needed for St. Clare's Chapel in Berea, and donated the furniture as a small token of his appreciation for Father Beiting's missionary work.

Beiting also met the Hurst family who lived in Willala, off the beaten path from Mt. Vernon.[40] George and Francis Hurst had eight children, and Father Beiting said Mass in their home, using the kitchen table for an altar. "The family had two devilish kittens that often ran around the altar-table or climbed up its legs, which sometimes ended up with one of the children chasing them, making it quite an exciting liturgy, to say the least," he later recalled. "This was a different kind of worship experience."

Beiting fell in love with this large, happy family that reminded him so much of his own. Over the next five years, his relationship with the Hurst children became quite close, as he watched them grow with an almost fatherly pride. It was the beginning of a long friendship that has lasted to this day, even though the Hurst family later moved to Florida.

One of Father Beiting's first tasks in Mt. Vernon was to find a place for Sunday services. Behind the facade of this quiet little community, religious intolerance was evident toward the priest and the few Catholics in the area. Even non-Catholic people, who were willing to help whichever way possible, had difficulties as they received threats and ridicule from their neighbors. This became a frustrating situation, and it was nearly impossible for Catholic families to worship under those conditions. However, when Beiting met Pop and Mary Reynolds, they graciously offered the living room of their house for religious services.[41] For several months, Mass was held in the Reynolds home. But other worshipers felt uncomfortable imposing on this family.

Mr. and Mrs. Reynolds owned a snack bar, which was closed on Sundays, and Father Beiting asked them if the backroom could be used for Mass.[42] "It was quite bold on my part, but the Reynolds family, especially Mary, had pledged to serve the church and they wanted to see services continue in their community," he wrote years later. Shortly thereafter, people threatened to stop coming to the snack bar if the Catholics kept on worshipping there. Pop Reynolds, who was a kind and good man, told them that Mass would continue to be held in his snack bar. The Reynolds' rode out the storm of prejudice, but their business was never the same. Father Beiting always remembered their sacrifice, and to this day is grateful for all they had done.

By 1955, Beiting was working each day to help many poor people in Appalachia. As individuals and families continued to leave the area, poverty in the mountain region was still thirty percent higher than in other parts of the country, with an increasing number of needy people calling out for help. Hope for the poor that remained in Eastern Kentucky, was very limited because of poverty's escalating unpredictability. They were vulnerable to the deteriorating conditions of the economic, social, and physical environment that led to despair and futility. Indigence became their trademark, even though they were not living in poverty by choice. Yet, circumstances which were out of their control threw them into desperate situations that appeared insurmountable.[43]

During the last half of the 1950s, newspapers brought national attention to the plight of the poor in Appalachia. However, government was slow to respond and did not have the necessary research data to understand the vast and complex variety of uncontrollable problems throughout rural Eastern Kentucky, and other areas of Appalachia. Had our nation's political leaders visited this part of the country and viewed the discouraging conditions, they would have recognized the enormity of poverty's nightmare.

However, it was frustrating for Father Beiting to see the daily human tragedies of the poor who were caught in a cycle of unbelievable circumstances, affecting every fibre of their existence.[44] Many families continued to live in dilapidated facilities, which were unsafe and uninhabitable. Beiting met a widow who was living in an abandoned chicken coop, and a family that occupied an old school bus without electricity or water. One man's home was a broken down camping trailer with a collapsed roof, which he attempted to repair with a plastic tarpaulin. There was a family of ten who tried to survive in a shack with two small rooms. Elderly people had to walk a quarter of a mile for water. Father Beiting heard babies and children crying in anguish because they lacked food or suffered from disease. Winter was so desperate for the poor that even in their shacks, overcoats and caps had to be worn day and night.[44]

Even though Beiting gave generously to provide a better day for these and other people in need, he knew that this would not change their situation. He questioned the long-range implications of his work and realized he had to try something that would have a greater and lasting impact on the people. On one occasion, his feelings were reinforced while heading back to Appalachia with a carload of goods. He asked himself:

> *What good was I doing? Driving back and forth every week with a load of food and clothes did not solve anything. ...Poverty continued. ...The clothes wore out and food was eaten, yet people had the same problems they started with. ...I knew I had to do something more. All I did was feed people while they suffered in the shackles of poverty. ...I had to find a way to help them break those shackles.[45]*

When Father Beiting arrived home, he couldn't sleep. He felt compelled to identify his direction for the future. His objective was to initiate and influence change by helping people become more personally independent and interdependent with others in their community. To do this, he had to seek out and identify long-lasting solutions to the many needs of the area. Later in a meeting with the bishop, Beiting talked with him about his concerns. He said that his desire was to provide a more aggressive approach to help the people, by increasing the range, scope, and diversity of his work.[46]

Bishop Mulloy believed that Beiting's broad posture of service would be consistent with the Catholic Church's mission. Wanting to provide help, he assigned newly ordained James Wordeman in 1955, to serve as Beiting's assistant for one year. Subsequent one year-assignments were planned for other newly ordained priests, as Bishop Mulloy's desire was to channel them toward wanting to stay and work in Appalachia. Those that followed Wordeman during the remainder of the 1950s, were Joseph Pilger, Herman Kamlage, who had previously served as a summer intern, Leo Sudcamp, and John Goeke.[47]

Beiting never pushed his assistants to remain in Appalachia, for he understood the apprehension and stress of working in this type of environment. However, his desire to help ease their concerns uplifted them. Father Beiting's love for the church and excitement about priesthood became a lasting example to his assistants. Years later, Father Kamlage referred to his experience as "one of openness in human interaction and the freedom of each individual's ability to function effectively."[48] Above all, the young priests had gained a view of a wide range of experiences with both Catholic and non-Catholic people.

As Beiting looked at ways to bring about change, he knew that he must establish priorities.[49] First and foremost, expansion of his spiritual and humanitarian work implied that additional facilities were needed for the growing number of initiatives, and living facilities for more volunteers. This also meant a greater and probably irreversible involvement of the Catholic Church in Appalachian community life. Despite operating on a financial shoestring, Beiting knew that a building program would have a strong impact. As a result, he selected Lancaster as the center of his work, because this community had the greatest need and potential for human involvement.

His first building was a multipurpose parish hall, completed at the beginning of 1956. This facility would host programs, functions, and services for the total community. Father Beiting and an architect friend, Carl Bankemper from Covington, designed the hall. Bankemper worked gratis developing the basic design, and Beiting's father and brothers contributed their weekends to help him construct the facility.

At the same time, an increase in the congregation at Lancaster provided the impetus to build a new church. They had outgrown the three-room chapel, and living quarters for volunteers were also needed. Architectural plans were developed by Bankemper, who graciously provided services without charge again. As construction of the hall ended, the chapel was moved back a hundred and twenty-five feet to make room for the new forty by eighty-foot church.

Even though Beiting was able to raise some money, the financial situation was tight and he could not afford to hire the services of a contractor to do the work. This did not deter him from pursuing his objective. He bought building materials reasonably from a parishioner and hired a local man to help him weekdays. On weekends, his family and other volunteers went about the task of building the church, as the completion date was set for 1957.[50]

Starting in the mid-fifties, Berea faced a tide of visitors from throughout the nation, as the college celebrated its 100th anniversary, and many functions took place.[51] The development of arts and crafts shops, and exhibits, both through college and community efforts, began to transform Berea into a semi-resort haven. Visitors were looking for a place to go to Mass on Sundays, and it became apparent to Beiting that St. Clare's Chapel could no longer accommodate the influx of weekend worshipers. At the same time, he was planning for eventual implementation of programs and services for the poor and needed accommodations for volunteers. Over the next few years, an old barn behind St. Clare's Chapel was converted into volunteer living quarters. Also, architectural plans were set in motion for the future construction of a new church facility.

With the expansion of Father Beiting's ministry, the reticence that mountain people had toward him was beginning to reflect a change of attitude in the latter part of the fifties. His work with the summer Bible program for children brought an awareness about the importance of the spiritual aspects of life and social growth. Yet this was not enough for Beiting, because he wanted to expand opportunities and saw that poor children could do very little to enjoy life, especially during the summer months.

He initiated a plan that would leave a permanent imprint on them by developing a summer camp that included positive

Father Beiting with poor children enjoying happy summer camp experiences

learning experiences and enrichment activities.[52] However, to carry out this plan, he had to overcome another financial obstacle. The diocese did not have money to give, and expenditures were already allocated to the building of his first church in Lancaster, as well as future construction in Berea and McKee (Jackson County). After great consideration and soul searching, his sincere interest and caring for the children of poverty prevailed. In 1957, Beiting had borrowed money, and Father Herman Kamlage, his associate at that time, also contributed financially, and a piece of waterfront property on Herrington Lake in Garrard County was bought to start a camp.[53]

Beiting met with Bishop Mulloy and received permission to form a non-profit corporation called Cliffview Lodge. Though his personal preference was to call the camp "St. Joseph's Inn," Beiting did not want anyone turned off by using a Catholic-sounding name. He buried that desire in his heart, and decided that this camp should be truly ecumenical.[54]

The camp offered recreation and fellowship in a Christian atmosphere for needy children, and was racially integrated at a time when segregation had a stranglehold on society. Beiting remembered his work with the students at Howard University and meeting leaders of the black community in Washington, D.C. "I was determined that if the church was going to be a voice of prophecy, it had to be concerned about all people— black as well as white folks."[55]

Positive reinforcement of getting along with others was part of each child's daily experiences, for Father Beiting recognized that they came to camp with many problems. Volunteer counselors were his mother, Aunt Rose, cousin Mildred and her children, the Haragan family from Louisville, as well as seminarian interns. Each child learned about high moral and ethical values, as well as a sense of serving others. Results of the camp program were encouraging, and enthusiasm by the children carried over into their families and communities. Beiting hoped that each youngster would emerge with a solid foundation of positive qualities and continue to grow spiritually and socially.

An example of the effectiveness of this program showed up years later, when Beiting was visiting an auto dealer in Lexington, Kentucky. A young black salesman asked if he could be of assistance. Before the conversation could continue, the salesman looked at him and said, "You sure remind me of a priest I knew a few years ago, but your hair looks more gray. His name was Father Beiting, and I would just love to tell him about the things that have happened to me." Beiting acknowledged that he was that priest. Smiling with pride, the young man pointed to his picture on a wall with the heading "Salesman of the Month." He became successful after graduating from high school and serving in the Armed Forces. Throughout the years, he often thought about what Beiting told the children at camp that a great deal could be achieved if they really put their mind to it and gave people a chance to be of help. The young salesman thanked Beiting for his guidance and encouragement, which helped him get ahead in life.[56]

One of the things that stood out in Beiting's work was his ability to demonstrate the effectiveness of integration into community life.[57] For example, his programs, services, and activities were open to the black people as well, which made up about nine percent of Lancaster's population. The outdoor space at St. William Church was ideal for activities, and he constructed a couple basketball courts, a baseball field and football area. Along with the newly-completed hall for indoor activities, he created a comprehensive recreational complex, and was proud that these facilities were available for the total community, especially the young people.

Most of the youths that came to participate were black, since the church was located close to a section of town where they lived, called The Shoot. "This name was given to that area because it was noted for having a lot of shootings," Beiting remembers. "Most of these families were the poorest of the poor, and their children had nowhere to go for recreational activities. Often times, they did all kinds of foolish things, such as stealing soft drinks from the church hall or making mischief that escalated to malevolent acts."[58]

One incident that Father Beiting remembers to this day involved the taking of money from his office. The rectory was open to almost anyone, and he had a little television set in his office for the young people. At that time, Mrs. Rita Brockman, a widow who was one of his first full-time volunteers, and her children lived in a trailer behind the rectory. Her son usually came to watch television, and he had a habit of taking his shoes off, leaving them behind until the next day. When Father Beiting noticed that money had disappeared, Mrs. Brockman's son also realized that his shoes were missing. However, a pair of beat-up sneakers were lying on the floor. Beiting remembered that they belonged to one of the boys from The Shoot. He went to the youth's house with the sneakers and confronted him, but the boy denied taking the money or shoes. The boy's mother was very upset with her son, and gave him a good tongue-lashing. As a result, the money and shoes were returned.[59]

There were other kinds of problems Father Beiting had to face. However, he understood that having very little would sometimes make a youth lose perspective on life. Yet, his belief that all people have goodness in their hearts led him to encourage the young to change their ways, rather than have them punished. Consequently, he made them aware that responsibility was important, if they were to succeed as good citizens.

He told the youths that the recreation center was available for them to enjoy the activities, but they had to respect the church's property and everything else in life.

Father Beiting did not hold a magic wand over these youngsters. Each one knew they had to police themselves. "It was amazing how often they supervised each other to prevent wrong doing," he said. "If youngsters got out of hand, the older ones responded by making them aware they were not going to get away with it, even if it meant using physical restraint."[60] However, this very seldom happened, because they respected Beiting for his trust in them. The responsibility was theirs, and if they failed, there was no one else to blame.

Providing opportunities for these young people brought Father Beiting into greater contact with black adults. He received many invitations to speak at their churches. Ecumenical unity, racial equality, and anti-poverty action served as a cornerstone of this dedicated priest's ministry, and whenever he had the opportunity to espouse these causes, his voice was heard. Responses from the congregations were inspiring, as people continually applauded Father Beiting who took daring steps before integration and Vatican II came about. They liked what they saw in him—a man whose heart was open to all people, carrying out the work of the Lord with great sincerity.

During the latter part of 1957 through 1959, Father Beiting continued to carry out plans that helped shape his ministry for the coming decade. He constructed facilities to accommodate spiritual and humanitarian programs and services. The money he raised by writing letters to donors increased as he included more cities throughout the United States. He added speaking engagements to his itinerary, and the secret of his success was the ability to articulate the hardships of Appalachia's poor. Groups, organizations, clubs, and individuals from throughout the country became donors to Beiting's fight against poverty. Inseparable from these activities was his ability to persuade individual and corporate benefactors to contribute in-kind gifts to help the cause that he believed in. They were moved by his ideas on how to alleviate poverty and social injustice, and getting races and religions to work together.

By 1958, Beiting's friends and colleagues were worried about his health, because he worked so hard, stayed up late with only a few hours of sleep, and pushed himself endlessly. This earned him the reputation as a man on a mission driven by perpetual motion. He was racing against time, looking for ways to help the people.

To meet this objective, the development of facilities took precedence. With the church and hall in Lancaster completed, and construction to expand Cliffview underway, Father Beiting concentrated on the three other remaining missions during 1958 and 1959. Starting with Berea, the architectural plans for the new St. Clare's Church were completed. With the help of six brothers, who were carpenters and bricklayers, and his father as foreman, the construction of the church began, with anticipated completion by 1960.

While it would have been ideal to view all missions of his parish in the same light, Father Beiting approached each community's needs pragmatically.[61] With a grasp of practical considerations, he looked at Jackson County with its own unique needs. Convinced that the people should have a permanent place for worship, Beiting looked for land on which he could place a trailer to be used as a chapel. A few years later, he built a multipurpose facility, combining a church, rectory-volunteer dormitory and hall that would house a mixture of services and programs.

In Rockcastle County, Father Beiting found that the need

for a rummage store was an overriding concern for the poor. Such stores were successful in Berea and Lancaster, and he was aware that people needed not only food and clothing, but also help in other ways. He rented an old ramshackle grocery store on Main Street in Mt. Vernon, which required repair. After fixing the place up, Beiting opened a rummage store. It turned into a gem, becoming a community center where entire families gathered for companionship. "We had story hours for kids, evening classes for adults, and more," he recalls. "The concept of a community center was evident when people came into the store just to talk."[62]

The volunteers who staffed these stores were more than shopkeepers, and Father Beiting wanted them to be friends to the people they served. They combined work with caring for their customers. It was not uncommon for a person to leave the store with a pair of shoes, or a can of beans, and a spiritual lift. They had shared their problems with the volunteers, and as a result, felt a sense of belonging. "I think God blessed our efforts much for the companionship and gifts we were providing to His isolated mountain people," Beiting reflects. "After all, He was the one who said that man does not live by bread alone." [63]

On June 1, 1959, Father Beiting received a call from the diocesan office, informing him that Bishop Mulloy had died after suffering a heart attack. Beiting was shocked and saddened by the news. It was the passing of a man for whom he had deep affection. Mulloy, an innovator, never hesitated to take chances, and his strong concern for Appalachia's people was evident in the hospitals, schools, and churches he built. Through his leadership, religious communities and diocesan vocations were brought to the mountain region. Bishop William T. Mulloy was not content to have the Catholic Church hidden in some remote area of Appalachia. He wanted the mission located in county seats where the religious, like Father Beiting, were a visible part of society. By doing it this way, these missionaries could enhance communities and make them more special than they had been before. "He was a dynamo in getting things done and one couldn't help to want to emulate him in keeping that spirit alive," Beiting says. In a very special way, Ralph William Beiting owed a great deal to Bishop Mulloy. He recalled in later years the impact that this bishop had on the diocese, and on himself as well.[64]

> *If one looks at the Diocese of Covington and Lexing-*
> *ton, the major turns that brought them to where they*
> *are today were taken under Bishop Mulloy's admin-*
> *istration. He moved the diocese and essentially the*
> *Appalachian part of the church, as I don't think any*
> *other bishop in this century has done. He was a doer,*
> *and had vision. ...He told me on numerous occasions,*
> *"go out and do it; don't be afraid. Take a step for-*
> *ward; you will never get anywhere by going back-*
> *ward or standing still." I didn't always know the way,*
> *but he encouraged and motivated me to carry on. I*
> *deeply treasure his friendship and confidence he had*
> *for me. Above all, he had great enthusiasm for the*
> *church.*

As the 1950s came to a close, Father Beiting had established himself as a spiritual and humanitarian leader with an unsink-able faith in the worth of what he was doing. His efforts to bring spiritual enlightenment and alleviate poverty were based on carefully determined priorities. He worked steadily to de-velop services and programs, but limited resources were a major concern. However, this did not deter his direction because he felt that the church in Appalachia had to be ready to serve every human need—material and spiritual. "The only thing worse than telling a hungry man you will pray for him, is to give him bread and not pray for him," he said.[65]

At this time, Beiting's work was gaining attention in the region and other parts of the country. To help fulfill his dreams, he would have to tap the energies of a greater number of people to serve as volunteers. In expanding his operation further, Father Beiting was taking a step into the unknown, yet his initiatives in the fifties would serve as a strong foundation for many more programs and services.

Part of Father Beiting's preaching campaign on the Ohio River

CHAPTER V

ESTABLISHING THE
CHRISTIAN APPALACHIAN PROJECT

The 1960s exemplified a significant period in Father Ralph William Beiting's efforts to initiate change for the poor. Certain events played an important part in his founding of the interdenominational Christian Appalachian Project, as thousands of workers and volunteers, who were also concerned about the less fortunate, joined his crusade. As a result, Father Beiting brought to light positive experiences and motivated many needy people who were never reached before. His success in providing a positive direction for them, was based on a rational plan of action with long-term ramifications. At the same time, our government had also been raising many questions of how to fight poverty, however, federal action was slow, and it would take until the mid-sixties before the War on Poverty got underway.

In June 1960, newly appointed Bishop Richard Ackerman came to Berea to dedicate the recently completed St. Clare church. At this time, Beiting briefly informed the bishop of the desire to expand his missionary work. Bishop Ackerman was enthusiastic and suggested that Father Beiting meet with him to discuss his plans.

Father Beiting is shown here with his close-knit family during the early years of his priesthood

Encouraged by the bishop's response, he began to gather data and information. With the help of volunteers from Newman Clubs throughout Kentucky, as well as seminarians, a needs assessment survey got underway. Volunteers and seminarians went into the communities to collect information about interests, aspirations, attitudes, and opinions, by administering questionnaires to people, regardless of their race, nationality, or religion. The response was overwhelming and conveyed the spiritual and social needs in each community and how the Church could help. "Spiritually, they indicated a deep concern for God," Beiting recalls. "Some folks attended our church on a voluntary basis even though most did not become Catholic." As for social needs, a majority of adults wanted an opportunity to work, since many were unemployed. Other concerns came to Beiting's attention, but finding ways for people to gain employment was his top priority.[1]

After extensive meetings with parish leaders, Father Beiting began to assemble avenues of opportunity.[2] He knew that Appalachian farms played an important part in the region's existence, going back to the time of its settlers. However, through the years, agriculture had declined, and the land was no longer suited to grow many crops. Yet, Beiting envisioned that agricultural know-how mixed with ingenuity would lead to the development of small businesses such as a dairy farm, greenhouse operation, raising pigs, and growing selected crops. He also saw opportunities for wood product industries in providing employment as well as being profitable. Although these enterprises would not create a great number of jobs, each could make a small but significant impact on the local economy.

A series of meetings over an extensive period with Bishop Ackerman brought into focus Beiting's direction, and led to a maze of precepts involved in the planning of a private non-profit organization, and a critical analysis of its purpose. He made the bishop aware that Cliffview Lodge did not meet the criteria for a large multipurpose organization. The camp was successful, but Beiting felt that it was imperative to expand beyond the scope of this operation to meet the needs of all people. His plan called for an autonomous organization—the Christian Appalachian Project (CAP).[3]

However, the bishop stated that the Catholic Church was

unable to support such an undertaking financially. In order to avoid future problems, Beiting suggested that CAP become a separate entity from the parish, "This way the church is not obligated to maintain the organization." After further examination of the plan, Bishop Ackerman supported the mission of the proposed Christian Appalachian Project, and gave his consent. Functioning as an independent operation, this interdenominational organization would have its own board of directors. Father Beiting vividly recalls his discussion with Bishop Ackerman.

> The Bishop said, "I'm concerned about the poor, and if this is a way to help them, I give permission. I can give you no money nor can I promise you any personnel." I assured him that while I would like to have both, I was content with what he had outlined. On that day in Covington at the chancery office, Bishop Ackerman was ultimately responsible for the Christian Appalachian Project coming into being. It was my idea and I had done all the groundwork and strove to get the resources necessary to make it come about. If the Bishop had said to me, "I don't think it is a good idea, don't do it," I would not have done it.[4]

Even though CAP became a separate entity, it still needed support from the church. Personnel, and the use of facilities for housing of volunteers and workers were just two of the many in-kind church contributions. From the start, all resources of the fledgling organization were kept separate from the parish, and finances never intermingled.

Even though Father Beiting gave a lot of attention to planning the Christian Appalachian Project, he did so without compromising his spiritual work. In 1961, Bishop Ackerman appointed him Dean of the Diocese's mountain region. The story of how this came about dates back to the late 1950s. At that time, Beiting told his fellow priests that if the church was to develop and expand its mission in Appalachia, leadership should come from someone who could relate to life in the mountains. For years, the dean worked out of Covington, in Northern Kentucky, serving that role. However, concern had spread among the priests that there was merit to Beiting's suggestion.

In the latter part of 1960, at a meeting in Barbourville, Father Beiting expressed to his colleagues that he felt a new beginning for the church in Eastern Kentucky had come about. He cited the importance of helping all people, regardless of their religious background, and how this would create a solid foundation for spiritual and humanitarian work. Beiting also pointed out the significance of street preaching, and the home visitation program, to determine spiritual and social needs of the people. Therefore, it was recommended to Bishop Ackerman that he select a dean who would work and live in the mountains. The bishop replied that the request was reasonable, and subsequently, he appointed Father Beiting as Dean of the mountain ministry.[5]

Of the activities that engaged Beiting's talent and energy, he found street preaching most rewarding. In his new role as dean, he gave special emphasis to this type of evangelization. The bishop assured him that starting in 1961, at least fifteen seminarians would do their internship in the mountains each summer. As a result, Father Beiting established Lancaster as the center for training, and under his direction, the interns devoted five weeks to street preaching. The seminarians were divided into three groups. Beiting took one crew with him to preach in "out of the way places, in the deepest of no-priest land," where they lived in trailers, campers, and pick-up trucks. The second crew helped another priest with outdoor preaching in his mission parish territory. A third group did census work, traveled throughout given counties, and met with people to find out about their needs. During the five-week period, the seminarians exchanged assignments in order to gain a broad range of experiences.

At this time, Beiting's street preaching message to the people consisted of ecumenical themes that he still uses today. This was a change from the early 1950s when his talks emphasized the Catholic faith, purgatory, the Blessed Mother, the Eucharist, priests, and celibacy. Rather than enlightening the people at that time with these topics he found that this approach deterred their acceptance of his desire "to either reinforce their love for God or challenge their inertia to think about God."[6]

Even with the 1960s themes, which were based on common tenets of Christianity—God, prayer, family, and Christ's command to love one another—disruptive actions of people made some priests apprehensive about street preaching. For many mountain folk, this was the first time they had seen or heard a Catholic priest, and prejudice was not unusual in the 1960s. As the designated leader of the mountain deanery, Beiting understood his fellow clergy's concerns, but he was committed to street preaching and felt it was an important part of the ministry.

Even so, Father Beiting's own street preaching experiences were sometimes painful. He was shot at, hit by tomatoes, threatened with arrest, run off the road, and cussed at. Even some ministers attacked him verbally and spread evil rumors about the Catholic Church. At times there were black seminarians among his helpers, which led to another problem of prejudice. Labeled as pariahs, he stood up for them, and did not let racism prevail.[7]

On one occasion, in the middle of his sermon, a group of rough looking young men bullied their way into the crowd, cussing and threatening Father Beiting and the seminarians. At one point, one of the men unexpectedly grabbed the microphone from Beiting's hand and challenged him to a fistfight. This six-foot-two tall priest, built like a football player responded, "We've come to preach Christ, not fight with people," and took the microphone back. Surprised, the man and his buddies moved to the back of the crowd and threw firecrackers and bottles against a wall next to where Beiting was standing. He apologized to the audience for the disruption and continued to preach. After finishing his presentation, he told the seminarians to pack up the equipment immediately and wait for him in the cars, because he was concerned for their safety. As he passed the rowdies, one of them started to swing a chain close to his head. Beiting ignored him but said: "Well, boys, I'm sorry you had such a bad time tonight. Maybe tomorrow will be better." He then joined the seminarians, and they drove off.[8]

Probably the most telling result of Father Beiting's ministry in Appalachia was the comprehensive experience seminarians had encountered during the sixties, which proved to be extremely valuable for their future work. These young men gained insight of the hillfolk they never had before. After being ordained, some rose to the challenge and came back to serve in Appalachia. Priests like Jerry Stern, Jack Heitzman, Will Fraenzle, Frank Osburg, Joe Saulino, and Bill Poole helped make the mountain deanery the leading edge in missionary work. While not all seminarians returned to serve as priests in Appalachia, each one appreciated the work of the church in this region, and supported the missions in various ways. Some brought volunteers to assist Father Beiting. Others encouraged their own congregations to support the work of the church in Eastern Kentucky through money or in-kind contributions and prayer.

From 1962 to 1964, certain circumstances hampered Beiting's efforts to get the Christian Appalachian Project incorporated. The papers for CAP's non-profit status were in the hands of a lawyer who took an inordinate amount of time to accomplish the work. Beiting went to Bishop Ackerman and told him about the circumstances. He then asked if the properties could be recorded temporarily under the name of the church. The bishop understood the situation and gave his consent to Beiting's request. Finally in 1964, CAP officially received the Articles of Incorporation from the attorney, and the transfer papers were finalized.

A great deal of thought went into the name "Christian Appalachian Project." The Catholic social teachings Beiting learned as a seminarian, namely the encyclicals *Rerum Novarum* and *Quadragesimo Anno* of Pope Leo XIII and Pope Pius XI, were the foundation for his selection. The social nature of the church was very much on his mind, because of its intent to serve all of God's children. He further felt that the Christian Appalachian Project should be based on Catholic social values of life: a love for all people, regardless of their religious background, color, or nationality. Finally, his strong desires about the instructions of caring for the poor, given by the Apostle St. Paul, provided impetus to this Christ centered organization. Beiting succinctly explains:[9]

> *I called it "Christian" because I believed we had to be a spiritual organization. Without God, we couldn't last. The problems were too big. We'd get*

*discouraged. Only with our ideals firmly rooted in
faith could we persist and succeed.*

Furthermore, he felt deeply that the Christian Appalachian
Project should be an interdenominational organization, representing a diverse group of spiritually motivated workers and
volunteers, who would be committed to the cause of helping
the poor. He went on to say:

*It was obvious that there was more than enough
work to go around for Catholics, Protestants, Jews,
and any other believers who wanted to be a part of
our dreams. After all, we all worshipped the same
God.*[10]

Beiting chose "Appalachian" because this was the area he
wanted to serve, and "Project," since it would be known as an
action organization. He did not want to create a discussion or
political advocacy group that would lobby about issues. His
goal was to get people involved by "getting their hands dirty
and feet muddy." Furthermore, he wanted help from enlightened and dedicated persons "who would climb mountains, not
just talk about them."[11]

As founder and president of the Christian Appalachian
Project, Father Beiting was fortunate to have associate pastor
Terence Hoppenjans assist him in his work. Hoppenjans, assigned in 1960, was an important contributor for over eight
years in the development of the organization. He had previously taught at a seminary, and served as dean of discipline and
business manager.[12] Of the many associates Beiting had,
"Hoppenjans was the finest of the best and became the financial officer, who always reminded me that we had no money in

the bank, and I should not be spending what we didn't have. He was scrupulous that way, but I got us into a considerable amount of debt." However, they formed a friendship that has lasted to this day. Hoppenjans was a stabilizing influence, kept excellent records, and became a voice of reason for the many decisions Beiting had to make. He worked out of the headquarters in Lancaster, the center of activity, while Father Beiting traveled to the other missions in Berea, McKee and Mount Vernon.[13]

In 1963, Beiting gave considerable attention to buying land in Jackson County and completing the construction of a multipurpose facility in McKee, which included St. Paul Church, a rectory, and housing for volunteers. In addition, his work as head of the mountain deanery required much attention. A close relationship with the other priests was an inherent characteristic of his leadership, and he worked diligently to assist them. With the growth of new parishes in the region, he encouraged his fellow clergy to start with the "trailer-chapel approach." As these self-sustaining mountain missions were adding converts and his own parish congregations continued to grow, Father Beiting was always striving to balance spiritual and humanitarian activities.

At this time, Beiting introduced new elements to the Christian Appalachian Project's ongoing development. Building on the already present foundation of helpers, he selected individuals with leadership qualities for managerial positions. These people would assume important roles without high monetary rewards, yet, were guided by the desire to serve the needy. Selected were George Purcell, Melvin Marks, Dale Anastasi, Charlie Simpson, and Tony Licata, who worked hard for a fraction of what their talents could bring them in the corporate world. With these men managing CAP's first business ventures,

Father Beiting's economic development approach would be unique and interesting.[14]

Because of limited funds in financing economic ventures, Beiting had to be very creative in getting businesses started. Since his main source of income came from contributors who responded to his quarterly newsletter, it was obvious that he develop small businesses which required very little capital. By going in the direction of agriculture, there was just enough money for a down payment on his first venture—farmland. He also felt that each venture had to be flexible enough to accommodate the potential for offshoot businesses. To some people, this attempt seemed like suicide, but Beiting's ingenuity of making things happen was very evident when he started a dairy farm.

In 1963, he bought forty acres of land in Gray Hawk, the center of Jackson County, where it was not too mountainous and quite suitable for raising cows and pigs. Acquiring these animals for the farm came about in a unique way. The monks of the Trappist Monastery at Gethsemane in Central Kentucky had extensive knowledge of Father Beiting's work. When he visited the monastery in 1963, the monks promised him a few cows and pigs. They also made him aware that the Sisters of Charity of Nazareth, located nearby, wanted to donate some Holsteins. At the same time, a Catholic family in the Bardstown area contacted Father Beiting, and contributed two cows.[15]

Word began to spread about Beiting's initiatives to help the poor, and his newsletter reached many far away places. For example, in Syracuse, New York, a spirited group of high school students hosted sock hops and dances, and with the proceeds they bought a cow. Others sent contributions because of their enthusiasm and Christian spirit of wanting to help Father Beiting succeed in this venture.

Volunteers, who included members of Beiting's family, built a barn. Under the capable leadership of Appalachian-born George Purcell, who mirrored many qualities of Father Beiting, this business grew prosperous, and people were given jobs. In the latter part of the sixties, more land was acquired to include a commercial milking facility, which eventually became one of the best managed dairy farms in all of Kentucky. Later, CAP sold the farm to Purcell, who continues the operation to this day.[16]

With the need to make use of every bit of the purchased land, Beiting and his helpers decided that the timber-covered hillsides had potential for a logging business. Subsequently, he appointed Melvin Marks to head up the project of cutting the trees for firewood. By clearing the timber and selling it in the Lexington area, Beiting eventually established a sawmill. As a result, CAP bought additional timber land, and planted seedlings to grow more trees. As time went on, more timber was purchased from other people in the area, as this business brought employment opportunities.

Wanting to see the enterprise succeed over a long term, Beiting sold the sawmill to Melvin Marks, who employed local people and some of his own children. This became a successful operation. "Today, it is the only one left in Jackson County, as Marks and his workers provide a service that is not readily available in the area," Father Beiting proudly says.[17]

Another of Beiting's original group leaders was a young man with a broad vision, who came to the University of Kentucky to study agriculture. Dale Anastasi, a native of Lockport, New York, believed that to create economic stimulation in Appalachia, specialized agriculture was needed. After receiving his Master's degree at the University of Kentucky, Dale returned to work with Father Beiting, and devised new techniques and approaches in alternative agriculture. Years later, Dale started his own greenhouse operation, which became the largest complex of its kind in Eastern Kentucky, providing employment for people in need.[18]

There was still another venture that Beiting had in mind and also proved to be successful—wood products. Charlie Simpson, a native Kentuckian, came to the attention of Father Beiting with his ideas and interest in this venture. In order to get the business started, Beiting traveled to Cincinnati and persuaded some friends to donate used woodworking equipment. He and his volunteers built a facility on a segment of the property that CAP acquired in Gray Hawk, turning it into a woodworking shop. Charlie Simpson took charge of this operation, which made bookends, chopping blocks, candlestick holders, and other decorative items for homes and offices.[19]

This continued for a few years when Father Beiting, always scouting for new initiatives, met with a distributor of trophies from Lexington. "The gentleman made me aware that trophies had become big business and what he needed were fine wood plaques and standards of oak, cherry, and walnut that would be attached to brass plates and figures," Beiting recalls. "We were able to employ more people, as plaques and standards were added to our product lines." Years later, this venture was bought by Tony Licata, who was one of the original volunteers. Licata operated the business for a long time, then sold it to a larger corporation that still functions in Jackson County.[20]

Another economic development contribution on a small scale was Father Beiting's effort to initiate a cooperative working relationship with a large pickle corporation. Since some of his workers and volunteers were already growing cucumbers, an agreement was reached whereby CAP became a supplier to the pickle company, which opened a collection station in that area. Beiting encouraged others in the county to raise cucumbers as well, and sell them to the corporation. Over fifty families accepted his invitation, and they averaged a two hundred fifty-dollar income in eight weeks. This was significant, since the median income in the area at that time was slightly more than five hundred dollars a year.[21]

As the businesses got underway and people heard of Father Beiting's work, a gentleman by the name of Lee Patton approached him in the late 1960s about a venture of great potential. Patton wanted to make Christmas wreaths from pine boughs, normally thrown away by the timber industry. He had worked with a group of people in Barbourville, Kentucky, who assured him they could make 1500 Christmas wreaths that fall to sell to the Florida Junior Chamber of Commerce. However, Patton was informed that the commitment could not be met and he came to see if Father Beiting might have interest in attempting such a project.

Beiting called his managers and staff together, and Mr. Patton presented his proposal. "He was convinced that Christmas wreaths, made from discarded pine boughs, could be a product of beauty and provide other attributes significant to Appalachia," Beiting remembered. The managers had many concerns about jumping into this venture. First, there was no available facility for assembling the wreaths, and financial resources were limited as CAP was over its head trying to keep afloat. They felt it was too much to ask of this fledgling organization at that time. Yet, mixing common sense with spiritual desire compelled Beiting to develop the Christmas wreath workshop, knowing it would provide jobs.[22]

The most exciting part of this initiative was that Father Beiting found a way to get the business going. First, he had to locate a place to house the workshop. He traveled all over Jackson County inquiring among friends. One gentleman farmer, Ben Tinture, told Beiting that he had a tobacco barn, which was no longer in use, and offered it as a place to start. The barn was very open and purposely designed to let air circulate throughout, but would have been too cold to work in during wintertime. However, Beiting had no other options and decided to utilize the barn.

With the help of Ben Tinture and a group of workers, Father Beiting converted the tobacco barn into a workplace by covering the open spaces with heavy, see-through plastic to keep out rain, wind and snow. Gravel was spread on the ground, and one of Beiting's friends contributed damaged doors for use as tabletops, while workers built and attached the legs. Keeping the place warm was a problem, but Beiting found two furnaces from broken down mobile homes and a potbellied stove, which provided enough heat to accommodate the workers.

Despite the obstacles Father Beiting faced in developing this kind of business venture, he provided job opportunities to people of Jackson County, who needed work. Folks with no skills and little hope for a future came alive, as they gained employment. Other local people also earned a little money by selling bundles of pine boughs to the Christmas wreath workshop.

It didn't take long before the workshop proved to be a success. Within a few years more than 100 local people were employed each fall through the holidays, and a skeleton crew worked year round. During the Christmas season, homes and places of business throughout our country were decorated with wreaths made by the workshop employees. No one was certain, but CAP believed that this business became one of the largest direct shippers of fresh wreaths in the United States, and much success was due to the outstanding quality in the craftsmanship.[23]

There was no question that Father Beiting's economic development initiatives were beginning to make a difference, even though income was less than in other places of our country. The result of countless hours of planning and creating business ventures was evident in the enthusiasm and hard work of those people who were given jobs. Yet, Beiting knew that much more had to be accomplished.

In Berea, circumstances called for a diverse approach to economic development. One of the first projects Beiting undertook was to find a permanent home for the rummage store and expand its operation. Until the mid-sixties CAP was renting space to house the store in different areas of the town. Each time an owner sold the property, the store had to move, and Father Beiting felt that CAP should buy a facility that would be a permanent place for the operation.

At the southern edge of Berea, on U.S. 25, a complex of buildings was for sale. Its location in an area known for trouble, made the asking price very reasonable. Beiting saw its potential and, at a friend's suggestion, talked with the owner. Even though negotiations took many unexpected turns, they eventually agreed on a price.

Managing a rummage store in Berea called for someone with leadership qualities, and willing to take responsibility for major decisions. Doris Anglin, a German war bride who had moved to her husband Bill's hometown, would serve as manager. Though Mrs. Anglin accepted the position, Father Beiting had to convince her husband that it would be safe for Doris to work at the store, despite its location in a rough neighborhood. Beiting promised him that things would change with the clean-up and renovation of the facilities.[24]

Christian Appalachian Project workers began to reconstruct the buildings, and when it was finished, the complex looked very appealing. The grounds were well kept, and neighbors talked about the facilities with pride and appreciation. Bill Anglin was pleased with the outcome, and his wife Doris not only served as manager of the rummage store, but through the years set up similar operations in other communities. Her husband also became a strong supporter and often assisted his wife and Father Beiting. Doris Anglin worked with CAP until her retirement in 1995.

Beiting wanted to create more than just a rummage store in this complex and decided to call it the "Appalachian Village."[25] With the help of his family, workers, and volunteers, he added another building to accommodate the sale of furniture and appliances. In one of the smaller buildings, a volunteer started an electronics shop. There were three other little houses on the property and Father Beiting designed a plan to combine them into one large craft shop.

His enthusiasm did not stop there. He also came up with the idea of a building supply business. During this time, friends and others had donated a wide variety of materials and supplies. At first, much of this was utilized to construct buildings in the Appalachian Village and other CAP places. However, in the late sixties, donations increased as materials and supplies came from individuals and businesses throughout the country. This led Beiting to sell products at a reasonable price to help the local people and support CAP's construction projects.

As the Christian Appalachian Project continued to expand, storage space for goods, supplies, and materials was needed. Eventually, a large warehouse was built on the Village property. The expansion did not stop there, and in 1968, CAP bought a facility opposite the Village on U.S. Highway 25, to open a furniture upholstery business. With the on-going building and renovation, Beiting was determined that CAP should start its own construction company. Again, he saw this as a way of giving jobs to the local people, while insuring long-term employment through the organization's future projects.

Another important challenge for Father Beiting during the sixties was his continued effort to make sure that more children of the poor were provided opportunities to improve their personal growth. Even though the camp on Herrington Lake in Garrard County was constantly in demand, he felt that the needs of many children from other areas were not met. His plan called for the development of an additional camp located in Jackson County, where CAP owned land that was bordered on two sides by the U.S. Forest Service. In order to build a lake and a campsite, Beiting requested of the Forest Service a fair exhange of pieces of land. However, it became a long and frustrating bureaucratic waiting game. Time was of essence, since a dam for the lake had to be built before the rain season started. As the months dragged on without any official response, Beiting was upset, and finally wrote to U.S. Senator John Sherman Cooper asking for his help to get the matter resolved. In no time, the Forest Service responded to Cooper's request, and the properties were officially transferred.[26]

That spring of 1965, a group of college student volunteers came to assist Beiting and his workers construct three buildings on the campsite for use as dormitories. The camp, named Andrew Jackson, was open for a few months, when Father Beiting faced more problems, as two buildings were set on fire by a group of hoodlums. As a result of this incident, there was talk of discontinuing the project, but Beiting was adamant to rebuild the facilities and add a boat dock. In addition, canoes made by seminarians were available for people to use.[27]

Unfortunately, more tragedy was in store for Camp Andrew Jackson the following summer of 1966. People of the area came to the camp and asked if they could use the canoes and swim in the lake because there were no other opportunities for them in the county. Beiting agreed, as long as the rules and regulations were observed, while CAP provided a lifeguard. Everything went well until the end of August, when a teenage boy took a canoe out into the lake and disregarded the lifeguard's request to wear a life jacket. Reliable sources confirmed that the boy was "horsing around" when the canoe overturned and he drowned before help could arrive. Father Beiting was heartbroken by this tragedy, and offered the boy's family his deepest sympathy.

Almost a year later, Beiting, the Diocese of Covington, and CAP were sued for a quarter of a million dollars for the wrongful death of the youth. The trial was held in McKee, an area fraught with prejudice toward Catholics, which may have influenced the outcome of the lawsuit. Even though most people felt that the defendants were not at fault, which was well corroborated by witnesses, the plaintiffs were awarded fifteen thousand dollars. Concerned about the unfair decision and possible implications for future lawsuits by others, Clay Shackleford, an attorney and friend of Father Beiting, took the case all the way to the State Supreme Court of Kentucky. Over a year later the verdict came back, and all parties were found not responsible for the death of the teenager. While the defendants were unhappy with the cost of legal fees, it was the last time anyone in that area tried to sue them.[28]

The growth of CAP during the last half of the 1960s was not without consequence, and hard decisions had to be made by Beiting regarding increased funding of programs. Financial support was needed to develop new programs, along with existing ones that were expanding their services, to accommodate more people. In order to accomplish this, he had to create a new approach for raising funds.

Early in 1968, Father Beiting spoke at Harvard University. After the presentation, a gentleman asked if his brother-in-law, a fundraising consultant could contact him.[29] A few weeks later, Phil Sheets, from the consulting firm, visited with Beiting, and they discussed different marketing possibilities for CAP. He told Sheets he was interested mainly in expanding his direct mail approach to gain more contributors. Within a month, Gratian Meyer, president of the same fund raising firm, met with Father Beiting and suggested that CAP's potential donors should include people from all denominations. Beiting agreed, but realized that he was unable to financially undertake such a project because of the total cost. However, Meyer, a generous person, was willing to take a chance and suggested that Beiting pay for the postage. He would then defer the cost of the promotional material, mailing lists, work and expenses until CAP was able to reimburse his firm.

Appreciative of this proposal, Beiting spoke with Father Hoppenjans and told him that instead of sending out the usual number of letters, they would have to increase the amount extensively. Hoppenjans was very hesitant. However, Beiting expressed great concern about the many unmet needs, which CAP could not support with its present source of income. Even though Hoppenjans viewed the financial picture as not encouraging, he reluctantly agreed to take the risk.[30]

As Beiting undertook this new approach to fundraising, he insisted that the Christian Appalachian Project eventually take over the work done by the consultants. Consequently, this would provide an opportunity for employing more local people. As contributions gradually came in, initiatives for buying land, constructing buildings and getting resources to help a greater number of people became a reality.

A few years later, Ray Grace, who was the consulting firm's

account executive and eventually became president of Creative Direct Response, visited with Beiting to help solve a financial problem. He stayed overnight at the rectory in Lancaster, and the next morning went to Mass at St. William Church. Father Beiting's assistant at that time, who had not met Mr. Grace, was celebrating Mass, and asked the worshippers, "to say a special prayer, because we are in debt to this company and don't have any money to give them." Ray Grace was listening to this, and "how he ever stayed for the rest of the Mass was beyond comprehension, unless he understood that prayer was about the only solution to get back on course," Beiting later recalled. The Christian Appalachian Project was in great debt to the consulting firm. Yet, Ray Grace had confidence that Father Beiting would find a way to pay the bills.[31]

Concomitant with the growth of CAP programs and services, the number of volunteers increased during the later sixties. As a result, more living accommodations were needed. In Berea, Beiting bought a home next to St. Clare Church to accommodate more helpers. At McKee, the newly completed St. Paul Church multipurpose building, which included lodging, was already running out of space to house volunteers. When St. William School in Lancaster closed in 1965 due to low enrollment, the Sisters of Notre Dame transferred to another area, and Beiting redesigned the building to be used as living quarters for volunteers.

In 1968, Beiting built a large "state of the art" facility at Mt. Vernon with a rectory on one end and a volunteer dormitory on the other, separated by kitchen, dining and recreational areas. This was part of the new Our Lady of Mount Vernon Church building project. Beiting's father, who had retired from his job as superintendent of construction, volunteered to oversee the building of these facilities.[32]

With all four missions of the parish growing, Bishop Ackerman delegated an associate pastor to each church. One of their duties was to coordinate volunteer housing at the mission centers. Extra trailers were placed on church properties, and CAP workers built living quarters for volunteers on the two campgrounds. "Though accommodations may not have been suited for gracious living, we were too tired to know the difference, and as long as we had a bed to lie down on, this was the most important thing after a backbreaking, but gratifying day of work," a former volunteer said.[33]

When Father Beiting started the Christian Appalachian Project, he foresaw that volunteers had to be a major part in this organization's foundation. He knew that CAP could not run at top efficiency without the help of volunteers to support the many causes. They came to construct buildings, plant gardens, train people for jobs, teach children in ecumenical Bible schools, serve as camp counselors, wash dishes, dig ditches, and do other types of work.

At first, it was not easy to find men and women willing to work without pay or applause, but Beiting's recruitment of volunteers began to take a different direction. He recruited people through newsletters, college students, and personal contacts of family, friends, and organizations. The result of his efforts showed progress, as the volunteer program grew steadily.

As the scope and scale of CAP's services increased, so did the role of volunteers. College students, clergy and religious, retired people, and other concerned citizens came to work cooperatively. By 1966, volunteer service had mushroomed to one thousand, with most people participating during the summer months. When the federal government sponsored VISTA, and other service agencies were in need of help, Beiting turned away prospective volunteers. In 1969, as CAP's program reached two thousand, there were almost too many for the available work. In turn, the screening process became more exacting and the caliber and commitment of volunteers improved.[34]

A major reason why people from all over America came to work with Father Beiting was his commitment and dedication to help the poor. For those who joined his crusade, Beiting said:

> *When volunteers begin their work with CAP, we ask that they do not come to do their own thing. To create a favorable climate for volunteers, CAP has formulated a plan of what is expected of them. It offers in-service training that helps volunteers adjust to dealing with people living in poverty.*[35]

Volunteers also saw that it was not an easy task to help Appalachian children and adults achieve a better way of life. Confronted with the bitter reality of poverty, they understood Father Beiting's rationale for wanting the recipients of their help to become active participants in the process for change. They further realized that to assist poor people in carrying out the desire to break away from impoverishment, carefully determined priorities were necessary. For this to come about, volunteers were trained by CAP to recognize and draw on the elements of people's individual differences. In turn, the needy were provided with incentives to help create motivation and encourage self-discipline, which gave them confidence to deal with their problems of poverty.

When volunteers first came to Appalachia, most did not have full knowledge about the problems of the poor, and had to travel a demanding road to help them. Also, Father Beiting may have been harsh on some volunteers, especially if he sensed that they were not carrying out their duties to the fullest. However, they realized that he wanted them to do their best, and at the end of their experiences, they were able to see for themselves the vision of his goal. In many letters written by former volunteers, they told him that his firmness was necessary. Otherwise sadness and despair would have overtaken them by working with people whose economic and social conditions were so depressing. Yet, a most important lesson that volunteers learned was that Beiting exemplified selflessness and dedication in nurturing the poor to self-direct themselves toward a better life.

Years later, Father Beiting received a letter from Louis Freeh, who was a former volunteer during a summer in the late 1960s. He wrote of his appreciation for the spiritually inspired experiences that were provided through Beiting's leadership, which made him reflect on what his own future life should be all about. Today, he is the retired Director of the Federal Bureau of Investigation.[36]

In 1968, the nationally recognized Lane Bryant Volunteer Award called special attention to the profound effect that Father Beiting had on the thousands of volunteers who worked for his various projects.

> *Many came out of idle curiosity, all stayed far longer than anticipated, inspired by the raw need of their services and the enthusiasm of Father Beiting. He has given them an opportunity to channel their youthful idealism into hard work and accomplishment instead of frustrating, negative protest. Thus, in upgrading material life in Appalachia, Reverend Beiting has built a bridge, a spiritual bridge, between the well-to-do and the poor, young and old, educated and uneducated.[37]*

One of the most rewarding benefits that volunteers gained while serving with Father Beiting was the development of friendships with fellow workers. These new and varied friendships created a kind of camaraderie that had a lasting affect on many of them.

Years later, their mutual trust and loyalty were explained by Dale and Marie Anastasi at a conference in Berea. They reminisced about the impact that Beiting had on volunteers. His advice, wisdom, determination, and spiritual guidance were not forgotten when it was time for them to move on to other opportunities in life. The Anastasi's talked about fellow volunteers that became friends, such as Shamus Fitzgerald, a New Yorker, who remained in Kentucky, and succeeded as a respected juvenile judge in Louisville. Then there was Charlie Simpson, a former Appalachian, who moved to Missouri with his wife and children during the great exodus in the 1950s. Simpson had many ideas for woodworking projects that inspired Beiting to ask him to come back and help others, which he did.[38]

Dale and Marie Anastasi told of the good memories about George Purcell and his wife Wanda, who still live in Gray Hawk, Kentucky. A native of Lancaster, George was five years old when he attended St. William's School and met Father Beiting. Since then, their relationship became an enduring friendship.

Having grown up in Appalachia, George always wanted to help others in need. Through the years, the influence of Beiting's work blended in with his own dreams, and he also believed that strong leadership was important for improving the economic and social conditions of the people. Encouraged by his wife Wanda, a Berea College graduate, George committed himself to Father Beiting's cause and became the "sounding board for many ideas." He had the distinction of serving as both the first lay employee and manager with the Christian Appalachian Project. George Purcell eventually gained national renown in the dairy farm industry, where he helped create many work opportunities for needy people.[39]

The Anastasi's also made a difference for others in need. In the late 1960s, Marie (nee Fano) was a novice teacher at Catholic Central High School in her hometown of Canton, Ohio, and came one summer to work with Father Beiting. The impact of helping others left her with the desire to come back to the mountains as a permanent volunteer. Soon after she returned to Appalachia, Dale, who was working with CAP and had met her before, reintroduced himself, and they eventually married. The Anastasi's started a greenhouse business that gained an outstanding reputation in the industry. Blessed with success and encouraged by the work of Beiting, they gave to many others and provided jobs for the poor.[40]

Joining the volunteers during the 1960s was an ecumenical group of religious workers. Priests, preachers, ministers, nuns, and seminarians served side by side, taught Bible schools, street preached with Father Beiting, and helped needy people in many ways. They came from places like Oral Roberts University in Oklahoma and Notre Dame University in Indiana. Some religious workers even took extended leave from their jobs to assist Beiting. They included a Lutheran minister and his wife from Wisconsin, a Baptist preacher, and a Methodist minister from Ohio. Among the apostolic workers were the Holy Cross Sisters from South Bend, Indiana, Sisters of Mercy from Chicago, Benedictine Sisters from Peoria, Illinois, and many others. Covington diocesan seminarians, along with the Augustinians of Philadelphia and SVD's from Techni, Illinois, also participated. Even seminarians from neighboring dioceses came to help. A network of information had spread throughout the country about this ecumenical endeavor, and the dedication of the many different religious people became well known.[41]

It was at this time that a world-renowned spiritual leader, Episcopal Bishop James Pike, was made aware of Beiting's work. Bishop Pike came to speak at Berea College, and on his way out of town noticed the newly built St. Clare Church. He told his host, College President Willis Weatherford, to stop at the church so he could pray and talk with Father Beiting. Although Beiting was in Covington, Bishop Pike remained to pray. Afterward, he commented to President Weatherford that the church had a "special aura of spiritual greatness," which the community should be proud of. Later, Dr. Weatherford told Beiting of the Bishop's compliment and thoughts on poverty that he wanted to share with him. Unfortunately, Father Beiting never had the chance to meet Bishop Pike, who died shortly thereafter while visiting the Holy Land.[42]

Bishop Pike was one of many well-known people who came to Appalachia during the 1960s, wanting to gain an understanding of Beiting's work. Even government leaders had interest in learning why his fledgling organization was making inroads while many federal programs were running into obstacles that made them falter. Perhaps the most important outcome of Father Beiting's efforts was that he produced results for the betterment of the underprivileged, no matter how modest. He was ahead of his time in doing things way before the government became involved.[43]

When the 1960's came to a close, it was evident that the never-ending problem of poverty was being challenged by Father Beiting. Ever since he arrived in Appalachia, his goal had been to change the malignity of the region peacefully and constructively. Through his care and concern, many children and adults gained pride and self-esteem, which made a positive impact on their lives. As Beiting continued to pursue new horizons, he would create programs and services with the one underlying factor that they enrich the lives of the less fortunate.

Courtesy W. Brunner—Berea, Kentucky

CAP Family Center provides a diversity of services for adults and children reinforcing the role of the family.

CHAPTER VI

GROWTH IN SERVICE FOR THE NEEDY

In the 1970s, Father Beiting's concern for the needy continued to be a distinguishing feature of his work. Through his leadership of the mountain ministries, growth of the church was evident as spiritual influence increased, and more people gained values that included individual worth and human meaning. Continuing to seek answers to the region's needs, the Christian Appalachian Project evolved into a growing and dynamic organization, aimed at creating new opportunities of economic development and human services. It is amazing that this was done without federal or state funds being granted to CAP at this time. Going it alone was never a question in Father Beiting's mind. He wanted the organization to be innovative and without government constraints. The Christian Appalachian Project did not duplicate federal or state offerings. Instead, it filled the void left by government relief and welfare by providing programs and services aimed at helping people to help themselves.

During this decade, Father Beiting placed emphasis on helping more people gain employment as he expanded existing businesses and developed new ventures. CAP's energies and resources were devoted to a wide variety of agricultural enterprise, along with providing employment opportunities in the light industrial field (metal factory producing ornamental iron items, woodworking operation, etc.) Retail jobs were made available through the development of stores (grocery, drug, etc.), shops (boutique, ice cream, etc.), and other small businesses. CAP also expanded its "Attic stores" (formerly called rummage outlets) to a total of five in the area, enhancing the job situation.[1]

A bold economic development incentive that escalated in the 1970s was the unprecedented "transfer of operations" approach, which motivated individuals with leadership qualities to undertake managerial and eventually ownership roles. This was unique, because Beiting insisted that CAP create businesses while it remained a non-profit corporation with a human-service attitude. Once an enterprise became self-sufficient, CAP sold it, often to the original manager, and installment payments were made well within reach of a profit margin. After the transfer, CAP would guide the new owner through the many steps of running a business, which became an important ingredient for their continued success.[2]

By the late 1970s, CAP's commitment to these long-range endeavors showed positive results. Even local politicians realized that the nonprofit private involvement of this organization played a strong leadership role in providing solutions that went beyond the stop-gap approach taken by government relief or recovery agencies.

Another interesting approach by Father Beiting in dealing with economic development during the 1970s, was the financial assistance the Christian Appalacian Project made available to local residents, who showed potential in starting their own small business. This initiative provided a tremendous incentive for people who were given low or interest free loans. For example, one mountain craftsman with talent for carving wood bowls and ornamental items had requested financial assistance in order to purchase machinery so that he could turn his work into a full-time business. CAP loaned him the necessary money, and even helped find outlets for his products. A few years later, this gentleman was able to expand his operation that included an offshoot business.[3]

People came with different needs, some more basic than others. When two men had combined their efforts to clear and restore land for farming, they approached Beiting for help and received machinery and seeds. Their crops eventually were sold at the farmers market and other produce outlets. The opportunity to expand their agricultural endeavor brought them further benefits, and they bought more land for farm use.[4]

Father Beiting also aided people in other ways. One man, whose children's behavior improved through the help of CAP's human service programs, was so impressed that he decided to do something about his own situation. He approached Beiting who gave the man hope and purpose by helping him get started in business. Encouragement and motivation were two key objectives in assisting him to change from idleness to seek employment. Through spiritual and moral uplifting, he developed a sense of direction, using his talent to make children's furniture, and CAP staked him to the necessary equipment. As the years progressed, he developed a fair-sized operation, selling his hand-crafted items to stores in several states.[5]

These were just a few examples of how Father Beiting attempted to stimulate local business and employment opportunities during the 1970s. As with the transfer of operations approach, the people paid back their loans in small installments, which CAP then recycled into other worthwhile projects. With such involvement, Beiting's objective was to reverse the long-existing trend of Appalachia's resources being drained off into other places of American society. The positive results that came from this task gave Father Beiting great satisfaction. He explained: "Any time we stimulate a local activity that sells its products on the outside and brings whatever capital it can back into Appalachia, is a true economic accomplishment for our people. It also makes persons who are willing and able to apply themselves feel a sense of self-worth."[6]

Father Beiting felt that it was not enough to reach out and help people get jobs, but that communities also had to play an important part in revitalizing employment for the area. However, for many towns and villages in Appalachia, the 1970s was a time of dwindling expectations. One example was the small town of Camp Nelson, located on U.S. 27, in the northern tip of Garrard County. For years, Camp Nelson's existence depended on farm products and a liquor distillery. In 1972, the distillery moved its operation to Louisville. Subsequently, all other businesses in town ceased to function, except for a ten-room motel, grocery store, and a filling station. Despair reached a new low as only a handful of people in the community had a job that Christmas. At the same time, this town, situated at the base of sheer cliffs on the Kentucky River, experienced another problem affecting access to the community. The government had constructed a bridge that spanned the chasm, bypassing Camp Nelson, and its future seemed doomed.[7]

However, Beiting decided that Camp Nelson with its rich history should not join the ranks of other forgotten towns. Its historical value dated back to the time when Daniel Boone hid in a cave there after escaping from Indians who had captured him. The town later served as a port, shipping tobacco and whiskey to New Orleans, and during the Civil War, it was the first recruiting center in Kentucky for the Union Army. "The history of Camp Nelson is astonishing," Beiting said. "The entire breastwork of a Civil War fort was located across the river."[8]

Father Beiting talked with his staff about this new venture he wanted to develop. "Soon thereafter, property was bought through money mostly borrowed or begged," he remembers. "We got loans approved, mortgages signed, and the rebirth began." He then spoke with architect Paul Kissell from Lexington, who had worked for CAP over the years. Kissell liked the ideas and dreams for Camp Nelson, and in a matter of weeks, plans and blueprints were completed. CAP employees and volunteers were the first to pitch in, and people of the area joined them to help revitalize the community. By the summer of 1974, life started to come back to the town.

The new Historic Camp Nelson included a large campground, two swimming pools, a service station, a motel, a large marina, a restaurant, a music hall-theater, boat sales and service with a storage facility, a miniature golf course, and several specialty shops. There were hay wagons for tourists to enjoy rides and see the sights, and a petting zoo was a favorite place for the children. They also had a flea market and did not charge the people who sold their wares there. Included was a farmers market, where one could buy fruits and vegetables grown in the area.

The effect of this venture meant employment for nearly one hundred and thirty people from the community and nearby places. In addition, these activities provided an opportunity for recreation where there was very little before. Maintaining the policy of getting people started in business, the Christian Appalachian Project later leased the Camp Nelson operation to private management.[9]

Even though CAP gave emphasis to developing jobs, Father Beiting also wanted to expand human development services, because he knew that the complexity of poverty called for a greater diversity of initiatives to meet all levels of needs of the poor. He felt that by guiding economic development and human service programs in the same direction, people would gain more benefits.

In order to accomplish his objectives, Father Beiting attracted professional personnel from within Appalachia and other parts of the country. Aided by volunteers, they developed a comprehensive offering of programs and services. At first, it may have appeared that certain offerings were not showing notable results, and some CAP personnel expressed concern about "the slowness of change." But Beiting was patient, for he understood the Appalachian people and the many nuances of characterization that made up their culture. He responded, "Any form of success is significant, regardless how long it takes. To many people who work with poverty-stricken Appalachians, it is a heart wrenching task, yet patience and trust in God will help us gain the answers to overcome poverty."[10]

Inherent throughout Father Beiting's missionary work was the importance he placed on children. He believed that youngsters who came from persistent poverty should have a chance for a different and better way of life. Starting in 1972, CAP developed its first pre-school and day care center in the basement of St. Clare Church at Berea, which was eventually moved to a specially designed facility in the Appalachian Village. By 1975, CAP's early childhood centers were operating in three communities. Their purpose was to give three to five year-olds a wide range of learning experiences before starting first grade.[11]

These centers, licensed by the Kentucky Cabinet of Human Resources, motivated the children to be social individuals and enjoy learning, so that they could succeed in school. Persons that brought expertise, leadership and guidance to this aspect of human development during the seventies included Marilyn

Stefanski, Ellen Burke, Kathy O'Donnell Kluesener, Kathleen Ford Leavell, Peggy Weick, and Mike Morrissey. Records showed that they were able to raise the standards for countless children who went through this program, and made an excellent transition into public schools.

Summer camps for children, one of Beiting's earliest endeavors, experienced the need to serve more children in the 1970s, and CAP expanded the program to accommodate over 1,000 boys and girls each summer. Activities included more than just fun-and-game experiences as workers and volunteers provided instruction in handicrafts, a non-denominational approach to Bible study, and promoted good health habits and personal hygiene. The outcome of what these summer camps meant to many underprivileged boys and girls was later explained by Father Beiting. "It gave much satisfaction to see youngsters from deprived backgrounds really open up, blossom forth and come out during a camping session. Apathy and resigned-to-failure attitudes in Appalachian children were not inborn. We felt they were learned, and could be unlearned to some degree, especially in a summer camp."[12]

Working with Appalachian children who came from a disadvantaged background presented interesting challenges to Father Beiting's camp counselors. Many did not know about certain things that other children in American society were exposed to. Beiting remembers, "When these young boys and girls came to camp for the first time, some were amazed to see a water faucet. They grew up with no running water in their shacks or cabins, and had to get it from a well or nearby creek. Many children were ecstatic to see and feel the water rush out of the faucets. This excitement carried over into the shower, since they normally took a bath in a galvanized tub. These youngsters experienced a world they never knew existed."[13]

On one occasion, the counselors asked a young boy to take a shower. He did not know what to do, and they explained that he go to the shower, turn on the water, and soap and rinse himself off. The boy did exactly what they asked of him, but no one had told him to take off his clothes first. "The counselors realized that many of these children were not acquainted with what most of us took for granted," Beiting explained. "Much had to be done in educating the children about the basics of life." [14]

Summer Bible School had undergone enormous changes in size and staffing during the 1970s. Through hard work and tireless dedication of volunteer teachers, each year proved to be more successful and resulted in a tremendous increase of students. Under Kathleen Ford Leavell's leadership, the teachers traveled from all parts of the country to share their love of God with Appalachian children. Sister Peggy Rooney of Boston, Massachusetts, came each summer, and Sister Jeanne Roberge, from New Hampshire, brought along a group of young assistants who taught twelve-year-olds, and tirelessly supervised the recreation program. [15]

The staff also included Bridget Doctor of Miami, Florida, Sister Sue Bourret from New Hampshire, Jeanne Kreckler of Cincinnati, Ohio, Cheryl Landry, Jean Carson, and Jeanne Guillamette, who all came from Rhode Island. Kate Weigand, of Pittsburgh, Pennsylvania, took time from her role as CAP volunteer coordinator to teach a course of study. To preserve the ecumenical unity Father Beiting had started, these people, along with others, worked endlessly to develop this nationally recognized non-denominational Bible program. "Throughout all the years of its existence, there has not been one incident of offense toward anybody of a different faith represented in this program," Beiting proudly states. [16]

When CAP introduced its remedial reading program to people of the area, it had to challenge more than just apathy or lack of interest on the part of children. It needed to create an excitement about reading, which youngsters often did not find in their homes. Father Beiting and his staff recognized the importance of reading as a major step for underprivileged children to achieve success. Therefore, a group of volunteers, specially trained and experienced in this subject, made sure that reading became an exciting experience for the children rather than a boring or threatening school task.

CAP developed reading programs in a variety of settings such as the community-centered Attic Stores, including the one in Mount Vernon, managed by Father Beiting's mother. A section of each store contained children's goods, supplies, and books, which made it ideal for volunteers to offer programs and tutor individuals. Summer camps also provided opportunities for remedial reading. "Since some youngsters could not read signs or directions to guide them to various facilities or places on the camp grounds, reading classes came in handy," Beiting recalls.[17] "When children were helped, this brought on a change of attitude and a yearning to succeed. They even wanted to keep the books, and enjoyed reading them at home. Interestingly, some youngsters started their own little library." [18] Since it was difficult for parents to buy books, CAP played an important role by not only donating these to children, but also to adults, groups, and organizations.

Ever since Father Beiting came to Eastern Kentucky, he saw how impoverishment had created frustration in the lives of Appalachia's youth. Too many grew up with deep feelings of insecurity, rejection, and deprivation, which brought on many of their problems and tragedies. This led him to develop a diverse offering of programs and services for teenagers. An important initiative was to establish group homes for boys, by helping those who came from a troubled background of alcoholism, crime, and/or absence of parental concern.

Moe Mercier, then director of the Family Retreat Movement at the Center for Christian Living with the La Salette Brothers in Massachusetts, decided to come and work with Father Beiting. Mercier and others, including Bob Weick from St. Louis, were instrumental in planning the group homes, which proved to be a much better alternative to a very sterile state institution.[19]

While living in these homes, the boys were employed, learned a trade, achieved a high school education, practiced money management, and developed self-reliant and socially acceptable behaviors. Records showed that a very small minority of the young men who stayed in the CAP group homes ever became wards of the state again.

Moe Mercier and his wife Stephanie, also a CAP volunteer, served as house parents in one of the group homes. This was a rough experience for them, but dedication to CAP's Christian based values and philosophies, both personally and professionally, gave the Merciers and other staff counselors that necessary strength to do their job effectively.

There were other groups of teenagers Beiting was concerned about, and he began to initiate more programs and activities. With the help of his workers and volunteers, attention was given to those youths who developed along isolated lines and grew up resisting social activities. He created survival camps that emphasized primitive conditions, adventurous white-water canoeing, and other activities, under the supervision of qualified counselors, which proved to be successful in reaching these youths. In turn, they found that cooperating with their fellow humans brought satisfaction and self-identity in realistic situations.[20]

CAP also sponsored Teen Clubs that included groups such as the "Bishops." This club, under the guidance of B.J. Walthers, from Philadelphia, originally consisted of black teenage boys, mostly Baptists, but grew in size to include white youth and others of different religions. As with all CAP Teen Clubs, the Bishops participated in recreational activities, and functioned as a community service group helping the sick, needy, infirm, and assisting other folks in any way they could.[21]

Beiting's commitment to the youth of Appalachia increased further, when he expressed the desire to do something for the many deaf or hearing-impaired teenagers, who did not have the advantage of special services. This provided the stimulus for Ric O'Connell, another of his workers, to study at Gallaudet College, Washington, D.C., where he gained the necessary education to work with deaf students. Ric then started a program to help these teenagers along with adults to enjoy a more fulfilled life. Under his direction, the program gained national recognition. Deaf and hearing-impaired youth as well as adults from the region, state, and even Canada, came to enjoy the special camps and workshops at Cliffview Lodge that accommodated their needs throughout the year.[22]

At this time, Father Beiting made Ric O'Connell CAP's official state government liaison to the legislative and executive branches in Frankfort, to communicate up-to-date information on CAP's work in Eastern Kentucky. A few years later, O'Connell helped the deaf community of Kentucky gain support for a bill passed by the State Legislature, establishing the Commonwealth's first Commission for the Deaf.

Other challenging problems Father Beiting faced in the 1970s, were people with other disabilities who also needed assistance. Since government programs and services for these folks were limited, Beiting developed initiatives that would have an impact on them. He appointed Jack Heyne, a CAP staff member who had to use a wheelchair, as director of the disabled adult program. Since Heyne grew up in North Dakota, and had worked with that state's occupational therapy program, he came to Appalachia with first hand knowledge of how to help disabled people.[23]

With Beiting's blessing, Jack found ways of assimilating handicapped persons into CAP's activities. For example, a number of people became employed in "Attic Stores," a task they were able to handle, giving them a meaningful, worthwhile job and income. Heyne, who overcame many obstacles himself after being wounded in the Vietnam War, also provided help to many ex-servicemen from the area, and made local communities aware of the importance of CAP's offerings for the disabled.

A major problem of the 1970s was the hardship and pain experienced by many of Appalachia's elderly people. Often bypassed in our society, a majority of this group of citizens lived in isolated mountain hamlets, where loneliness and despair were even more acute. Many did not drive, nor was transportation available to those who lived by themselves. Father Beiting's concern for them led him to initiate a comprehensive approach to help the elderly. CAP included visitation programs for these people, as volunteers gave assistance, helped with housework, personal care, and other services. Transportation was provided for the aged to visit doctors, clinics, hospitals, grocery stores, relatives, friends, and senior centers. Also, many of the elderly folks occupied places that needed repair, and CAP workers were called upon to improve their living conditions.[24]

Unquestionably, a most sensitive task for Father Beiting during this period was to find solutions to the breakdown of the family. Having always been a staple in Appalachia's culture, many families were under great strain as joblessness created a change in the father's role. Unstable income and lack of direction increased the problems of spousal abuse and domestic violence, as despair often led a husband to turn to alcohol or drugs, venting his frustration on the family.[25]

Beiting began to establish shelters, as abused women with children in tow came to CAP facilities, where they received help. CAP offered them lodging, food, medical aid, and counseling, which helped many to get a new start. If reconciliation was a possibility, the professional staff provided continued counseling so that changes could come about. However, if a family was unable to reunite, CAP provided alternative services.

As an added incentive for parents to turn things around for themselves and their children, CAP built a comprehensive Family Life Center complex, located in Renfro Valley near Mt. Vernon, which served as a place for reunions and counseling. The center involved many diverse activities aimed at reinforcing family life as the source of strength. It also included recreational areas where families could enjoy outings in beautiful surroundings.

With the growth of human development programs, Father Beiting felt that it was important for CAP to carry forth a total commitment to help people improve their living conditions. In the 1970s, too many Appalachians continued to live in substandard housing, which was a problem for generations. Sensitive to the many deplorable living conditions of the needy, he expanded the home repair workforce.[26]

Beiting organized home remodeling crews and provided jobs to unemployed men. With the help of volunteers, they improved all kinds of housing problems by fixing roofs, replacing windows and doors, repairing porches, and constructing new dwellings. The demands were so great that crews could not keep up with the much-needed repairs.

In one case, the tin roof of a shack leaked so much that when it rained, the inside became soaking wet. There were also many cracks and holes in the walls, and the elderly woman, who lived by herself, tried to cover them up with cardboard to prevent snakes and other vermin from crawling in. With no insulation on the inside and the place too far gone, Father Beiting decided that CAP workers would build a simple one bedroom house for this person in need. She was very grateful for not having to worry any more about the rain, snow, wind or unwelcomed animals coming into the house. This lady finally enjoyed amenities she never had before.[27]

Even though his workers and volunteers in the Home Repair program came to the rescue in many situations, Father Beiting had some concerns. He knew that CAP did not have the necessary resources or staff to meet the housing needs of all people. As a result, the Christian Appalachian Project worked more closely with state housing services, private non-profit, and church organizations. Later, as Habitat for Humanity came about, it also joined forces with CAP and the other groups in the constant battle to help alleviate poor housing conditions.

When Father Beiting started the Christian Appalachian Project, he emphasized participatory management. He believed that for the organization to carry on effectively, input from the staff, workers, and volunteers was crucial. This influenced an open and receptive climate, where people worked in a healthy atmosphere and spoke their mind, without being fearful of reprisals for original or creative thinking. As a result, the employees enjoyed their work and took pride in the organization.[28]

Beiting's expectations and treatment of his staff became a determining force for their high level of performance. It is amazing that he built the organization on flexibility, yet with a clearly defined direction of Christian duty to getting things done through action. Consequently, CAP produced a succession of effective programs and services.

Another major reason why the Christian Appalachian Project succeeded in the 1970s, was that Father Beiting had been able to recruit a nucleus of administrative personnel to serve in leadership roles, as the organization experienced a decade of expansion. Many committed themselves for a long time, and still continue the tradition of service.[29]

Having taken a methodical approach to recruitment of his top administrative staff, Beiting hired Bill Begley from Florida in 1971, to assume the duties and responsibilities as field director. With the increase of staff workers and volunteers, Mike McLaughlin from Ohio, was hired in 1974, to serve as personnel director. A few years later, he was appointed executive director. Joining CAP in 1978 was Reverend Jack Morris. Raised in the Ozarks of Missouri and having served as pastor for a rural congregation of the Disciples of Christ, Morris was appointed director of the human development programs.

Some of the other administrators Father Beiting recruited, who helped influence CAP's work, were Lew Phillips, special projects manager, Len Spangler, director of the Family Life Center, Sister Lyn Herley, director of the spouse abuse shelter program, and Rita Conley, emergency shelter program director. Unique among the people who joined Beiting was Peggy Gabriel, a second generation volunteer, who assumed a variety of administrative duties that were important to the organization's growth.

During this decade, Appalachia benefited from CAP in many ways, as people had an opportunity of employment with the organization. The advantage of its presence in communities made living conditions more desirable. As an effective antidote to community stagnation, CAP helped increase local revenue, and created an overall economic uplift. In Lancaster, where Beiting developed the administrative center, CAP became the largest private employer in that county.

Also, in the 1970s, Father Beiting's role as Dean of the Covington diocese mountain ministries intensified. When he accepted this assignment in 1961, the Catholic Church had served a very small percentage of the population in Appalachia. His tireless efforts to increase the presence of the church were very evident. With the help of other mission-minded priests, he set a goal of having at least one Catholic church in every county of the mountain deanery. He gained acknowledgment for his leadership, when Pope Paul VI made him a Monsignor on May 12, 1971. This honorary title was given to Father Beiting based on Bishop Ackerman's recommendation, citing his outstanding service to the church.[30]

Beiting enjoyed an active and vibrant relationship with the priests of the mountain deanery. He encouraged them through cooperative action, which became a positive force in helping to make their struggles less difficult. For instance, he provided help by raising funds to buy land and build churches.

Among those that Beiting assisted was Father Hoppenjans, his former associate and friend, who looked for property in Pike County to build a church outside Elkhorn City. He was able to raise money for the construction of the facility, which included a combined rectory and hall. At Booneville, in Owsley County, Father Wilfred Fraenzle received help to purchase land. Beiting went on a fund raising tour and collected enough money to buy a large trailer for use as a chapel. Years later, a church was constructed with the help of the Catholic Church Extension Society, and the trailer became living quarters for the sisters who worked in the area. He also assisted Father Thomas Imfeld in finding property at Stanton, in Powell County.

Beiting's architectural skills came in handy as he helped design the church, and raised funds for its construction.[31]

Most notable about Beiting's leadership quality was his openness to listen to the various viewpoints of other clergy. He felt strongly that his purpose was to recognize and support their meaningful work. This encouragement gave many priests the incentive to want to succeed in their ministry, and knowing that they could count on him inspired them further.

However, the conditions under which priests had to serve, and the many problems they faced, were too difficult for some to overcome. Subsequently, a number of men in the diocese left the priesthood, a trend that became common throughout the country. One of Father Beiting's friends, a pastor in Jenkins, decided to leave the priesthood.[32] Upon hearing of his intention, Beiting drove to Jenkins to talk to him. "Working in the deepest part of Appalachia played an important part in his decision. He was still excited about the priesthood, yet living in an environment so desolate, and being alone with no one to turn to, was unbearable for him," Beiting said. The young priest told him, "I don't know how in the world you put up with it. You have been here longer than anybody, and yet you keep on going." He felt that people didn't care for the poor of Appalachia. Father Beiting tried to convince him otherwise, but could not change his friend's mind, who eventually left the priesthood.

Every Christmas thereafter, Beiting received a letter from him, and a few years later was informed that he married a former CAP volunteer. "He asked if it would ever be possible for a married man to be a priest, for he still had it in his heart to be one," Beiting said. "I felt so sorry for him, because he was such a fine person. It was the loneliness and discouragement that made him leave."

Father Beiting showed empathy for priests who were struggling with their vocation, and remained a true friend, no matter what their decisions. As years went by, the number of priests declined, and associate pastors in the mountain region were almost extinct. Eventually, a mission parish consisted of only a pastor to administer to the people.

During the 1970s, Beiting's reputation continued to grow, and invitations to speak throughout the country increased. In August of 1973, he took his street preaching to the west end of Newport, Kentucky, for a revival at the request of Father Anthony Deye, Pastor of Corpus Christi Church. Large crowds gathered for the day and evening sessions to hear Father Beiting, who considered this something of a homecoming, having been born in Newport and baptized at this church.[33]

Also, in 1973, Father Beiting received the "Good Samaritan Award" given by the National Catholic Development Conference. The award was for his outstanding work as "a person who truly cares for his fellow people and gives himself to better others." He felt privileged, since Mother Teresa of Calcutta and other distinguished persons had been previous recipients of this award.[34]

In 1974, the tragic death of Father Tom Lubbers profoundly affected Beiting, who had high hopes for this priest as a spiritual and humanitarian leader. Lubbers, who had served as an intern and later as associate pastor to Father Beiting, was riding his motorcycle back to Lancaster after celebrating Mass in McKee. As he traveled down the Big Hill mountain road, a truck turned directly in front of him, making it impossible for him to stop in time. Father Tom was killed instantly. Father Beiting was heartbroken because he cared deeply for this young man who mirrored much of his own outlook on working with the people of Appalachia.[35]

It was during this time that St. Clare Church experienced a significant increase in parishioners. A major reason for this was the industrial growth in Berea, which created employment opportunities, and people came to work and live in the area. Realizing the long-term implications of the situation, Father Beiting made a recommendation to Bishop Ackerman that in order to better serve the increasing number of Catholics, there was a need to divide the parish. Thus, in 1976, a new pastor was assigned to St. Clare Church in Berea, and it became a separate parish with McKee serving as a mission center. Beiting would continue as pastor of St. William parish in Lancaster and Our Lady of Mount Vernon in Rockcastle County.[36]

Shortly thereafter, a journalist asked him about his greatest achievement in Appalachia. Without taking time to ponder, he answered succinctly, "Volunteer service." In order to understand Beiting's response, one has to realize that throughout the years, volunteers were a major force for bringing his dreams to reality. "Volunteers represent an endless source of new and vibrant ideas," he said. "Many of the human development programs, which have become most important to CAP and the areas it serves, were developed by volunteer initiatives."[37]

For example, Marilyn Stefanski, a former nun, came to CAP in order to continue to work in a Christian community. "Although Marilyn was leaving her religious order, she still wanted to serve God and His people," Father Beiting recalls. Stefanski worked as his secretary, then as a rummage store manager, and director of a child development center. She realized that there were a number of young children with disabilities who did not receive help from any other group or organization. This prompted her to obtain a graduate degree in Special Education from the University of Kentucky to meet these needs.[38]

Stefanski began a homebound teaching program, passing

on her professional expertise to disabled children and their parents. Her original approach of working in the homes was a huge success, especially for parents who realized that they were able to help their children in many ways. In 1978, the effectiveness of this approach led to the program "Parents Are Teachers." Since its beginning, many disabled children had reached their greatest potential. The significance of Marilyn Stefanski's work further highlighted the fact that this was one of the first such programs in the state of Kentucky. "Without her, it would not have come about," Beiting said. "She gave back to God some of the gifts that were bestowed upon her."[39]

There were other creative ideas initiated by volunteers. One young woman, Maryann Crea, was working in an Attic Store when she began to send notes to people who contributed clothing and other goods, asking if they would like to adopt a family at Christmas. The result of her letter made it possible for nearly 300 families to receive food, clothing, and toys that year. Eventually, this program provided baskets for nearly 3,500 families and elderly people for the holidays.[40]

Volunteers also brought a certain flair of spirit to their work. One of Father Beiting's favorite stories tells of another volunteer who built a spiritual bridge between religions.

> *We had a Baptist girl, Wanda Brannon from Alabama, who was a joy to be near. Everywhere she went, the contagiousness of her smile followed. When asked how she could be so happy living and working with people of different religious backgrounds, she smiled and said, 'We all have the same Lord and see him in all the people we care for.' She made being of a different faith an asset, not a source of contention.[41]*

Father Beiting's life was not always of a serious nature, for he had another side to him that included a good sense of humor, which showed in different ways. He could be a practical joker who took delight in sending volunteers after "board benders or sky hooks," or hide suitcases in trees.

Once, a young volunteer worked late into the night, and came home very tired. He took a shower and went quietly to the bedroom. It looked like his roommates were sleeping, and out of courtesy, he did not turn on the light and tiptoed in the dark over to his bed and laid down. Suddenly, he felt something strange under his body. He jumped up, turned on the light, and shouted, "I'm going to beat up the culprit who put corn flakes in my bed." His roommates roared with laughter and one of them told him, "You can't beat up on a priest!"[42]

Many humorous things have also happened to Father Beiting, where he was the recipient of something with a climactic twist. Father Lou Brinker, one of his dearest friends, told of an occasion when a group of priests gathered at a local lake. Beiting was taking pictures of them, standing near the edge of a boat dock with his back to the water, while trying to focus the image of the smiling priests. Led by Father Brinker, the group encouraged him to back up a little. He fell into the lake, holding the camera high above his head. Explosive laughter came from the priests as Beiting found himself standing in the water, continuing to take pictures.[43]

When Father Beiting started his work in Appalachia, he had the vision to see the importance of recreation as a necessary part of CAP's services. He made people aware about the natural beauty of their surroundings, and developed recreation programs for children and adults, based on a philosophy aimed to improve their lives with positive activities. Even though he grew up during the Depression, his own childhood included a well-rounded background of recreational experiences. Later, when Beiting attended the seminary and came home for a summer, he and his brother Don built a boat and took it for a two week excursion on the Ohio and Kentucky rivers.[44]

Father Beiting always had a soft spot for boats. Former intern, Father John Rolf, told how Beiting gave him and other seminarians a boat kit, and their assignment after hours was to complete it by the end of that summer.[45] This boat, and many others built by seminarians and volunteers, were eventually used by children and adults at the camps. "The boat rides were true eye openers especially for the children, and these experiences made them appreciate the natural beauty of God's creation," Beiting said.

Knowing of Father Beiting's long-standing interest in providing recreational opportunities for the underprivileged, his parents donated some money to CAP toward a downpayment for the purchase of a fifty-eight foot houseboat in the fall of 1977. In addition, Beiting took out a personal loan, and the president of the boat company as well as others helped with generous contributions. In 1978, many indigent children and adults, senior citizens and the handicapped enjoyed recreational activities they never dreamed of experiencing. Because of the need to also accommodate children and adults in wheelchairs, Beiting was able to trade the boat in for a bigger sixty-eight foot long aluminum structure, for practically no extra cost.[46]

Again, the Somerset Boat Company President, Jim Sharpe, graciously made a sizable contribution, and the Mercury Outboard Motor Corporation of Fond Du Lac, Wisconsin, donated the motors. Father Beiting explained to corporations and individuals what he was doing and additional help came for the cost of running the boat. The Ashland Oil Company sent a generous check, and others contributed furniture, equipment and money.

In the spring of 1979, the new houseboat was christened *Daniel Boone*. The maiden voyage took place as a group of boys explored the 200th anniversary of Daniel Boone's travel through Kentucky. Father Beiting proposed that the first leg of the trip start at the North Fork of the Kentucky River and continue to Cincinnati. The second leg would begin at Cincinnati, going down the Ohio River to Cairo, Illinois, on to the Mississippi River. When Beiting presented this idea to CAP volunteers, they were far more enthusiastic than he had anticipated. They felt it was a great idea. "Many of the kids worked hard and deserved a reward, while some needed a stimulation, and with others an opportunity was warranted," he remembers.[47]

The young people that made the trip were ten to eighteen years of age, and the crew included Father Beiting, along with several volunteers. There were eighteen boys on the first leg, and fifteen on the second, who represented a cross section of the Appalachian scene, consisting of black, white, Protestant, Catholic, and non-religious. Children with disabilities were also part of the group. Years later, Father Beiting explained his rationale for this trip.

> *I felt strongly that we needed to reinforce this sense of getting along, and how to make their lives fit in with others. ...The trip was a great step in that direction. I also wanted them to know and experience something of the outside world.[48]*

This excursion gave the youths a sense of appreciation for the beauty of Appalachia, and they experienced the challenge of such pioneers as Daniel Boone, James Harrod, Benjamin Logan, Simon Kenton, George Rogers Clark, and others. Beiting hoped this learning activity would encourage the boys to reflect on their own lives, and enable them to accept challenges.

As a life long student of history, Beiting came quite naturally upon a deeper interest in Daniel Boone, which prompted him to write *Soldier of the Revolution: a New View of Daniel Boone*, and *Adventures of Daniel Boone*. When he was asked how he had been able to write a book with such a demanding and full schedule, Beiting smiled and said, "I was nearly tempted to call the life of Daniel Boone "The Midnight Cowboy," as most of the writing was done after the other duties of the day were completed."[49]

By the late 1970s, his reputation as a spiritual and humanitarian leader gained national attention, but he also received recognition as the "traveling street preacher." Few priests had ever conducted as much street preaching as Beiting with such success. In fact, he was considered without a peer in this type of evangelization. From the time he came to Appalachia until the end of the seventies and beyond, his street preaching took place every summer with unfailing regularity.

By now, he had built a greater spiritual bridge between more people and himself through street preaching. News of his many sojourns into the back country had spread throughout Appalachia, exciting those individuals who wanted to receive the power of God and rekindle their religious flame. By doing this, Beiting continued to open doors for other priests to breathe new spiritual life into communities that were stagnating.

Father Beiting had high hopes for the future, but circumstances changed his immediate plans. When his mother had a severe heart attack and was ill over a long period, he visited her as often as possible. In addition, much of his time was consumed by speaking engagements throughout the country, raising a greater awareness about the Christian Appalachian Project and the problems that existed in the mountain region.

In 1978, Beiting had overextended himself in trying to shoulder too many responsibilities. On numerous occasions, Bishop Ackerman expressed his concern for Beiting's health, since he ended up in the hospital every so often from sheer exhaustion. The bishop even suggested that he take a rest and work in a less stressful place. However, Father Beiting reassured him that he was in good health and wanted to continue his ministry in the mountain country, where he felt the greatest challenges were. After one of his extended speaking tours, the chancery office called and informed him that Bishop Ackerman planned to retire. It was a time of sadness for Beiting, since he was very close to the bishop, who had been a strong supporter for his cause.[50]

Before the selection of a new bishop, Beiting was reluctant to be away from his work in Appalachia. However, his schedule continued to be very hectic even without speaking engagements in other parts of the country, and he seriously considered resigning as Dean of the diocese's mountain region.

Before making a decision, Beiting wanted to reflect on his situation and asked for a week's vacation, since he had not taken one in a long time. Incapable of saying no to requests, he included a couple of speeches in Florida during that week, but spent the remaining days by himself. A camper, a small boat, the water of the Caloosahatchee River, and the warm weather in February did wonders for him.[51] "The tiredness went away, and the tensions were gone. As I sat on the boat at evening time, I began to discover things I should have known. There was the exhilaration of a gentle breeze, water lapping against the boat, an afterglow of a setting sun, and the beginning of a starry night that brought peace and contentment," he recalls.

As Beiting had time to reflect, he began to talk to God about almost anything, including the beauty of His creation. "I wanted Him to know that I thought He was very special," he said. "And

I thanked Him for His love and the thousands of little things that made up my life. This was a time of relaxation and recreation, and it brought into focus my direction for the future."

After returning from his vacation in 1979, he met with the new bishop, William Hughes, and resigned as Dean of the mountain missions. Beiting felt that he had held the position long enough, and it was time for someone else to serve in that capacity. He had few doubts about himself as Dean and what he believed in. His leadership was a steady course toward the goal he always faithfully embraced. At age 55, his tireless energy continued within him. He was a man of perpetual motion, still burning with ideas and initiatives, and looked forward to the 1980s with great optimism.

Courtesy Christian Appalachian Project

Children enjoying water activities at one of CAP's camps.

CHAPTER VII

EXPANDING THE HORIZON
THROUGHOUT APPALACHIA

In the 1980s, Father Beiting faced a new challenge when Bishop William Hughes asked him to head missions in other parts of the mountain region. With the Church sending him to further develop Christian communities, he also initiated CAP programs in these places. Beiting's cause continued to be profoundly idealistic, yet extremely practical, as his efforts to help a greater number of people led the Christian Appalachian Project to experience unimaginable growth. As a result, a far-flung network of dedicated religious and non-profit groups were organized, allowing CAP to influence the fight against indigence throughout the thirteen Appalachian mountain states and beyond.

In 1980, Father Beiting celebrated his 30th anniversary as pastor of a parish that included Garrard, and Rockcastle counties. Through the years, these mission churches experienced growth, and were regarded as warm and giving congregations that drew strength and a sense of common purpose from this charismatic priest. This was a parish where people put their faith in the providence of God, and followed Christ, by actively participating in doing good deeds for the community, especially the poor.

To grasp the dynamics of Beiting's impact not only on his parishioners, but others as well, one must understand that his ministry combined spiritual and humanitarian action. For example, through his ecumenical work, he influenced clergy of other religious organizations to open up their ministries to meet the needs of each community. His strategies for ecumenism were simple. He hoped to create a movement that was morally sound and non-threatening to any religious organization, with people of goodwill working together. Even though there was some resistance, his efforts proved successful in bridging gaps that had existed for many years.

Father Beiting's influence also went beyond the local communities of Appalachia. Those religious volunteers who served under his guidance often called upon him for assistance in organizing and developing missions in the U.S. or overseas. Beiting's style of operation was often evident. For example, Father Jack McGuire, who was working in the slum areas of Cali, Colombia, invited Father Beiting in the early 1980s to advise him on the expansion of outreach offerings. His visit helped create new initiatives that included medical and dental services for those people who could not afford such care.[1]

During this time, acknowledgment of Beiting's overall contributions was further recognized by the many awards and honors he received. At commencement exercises on May 24, 1981, Berea College granted him the honorary degree of Doctor of Divinity, given in the spirit of admiration and gratitude for his years of dedication to Appalachia's needy people. The citation said, "Father Beiting's sense of compassion and an all-encompassing service could not be contained within the spaces of those churches." Beiting had great respect for Berea College, which gave much emphasis to working with local communities. In his Baccalaureate address, he exhorted the graduates to accept the challenge to work among poor people and provide leadership that was direly needed in Eastern Kentucky. Many were favorable to the invitation, and some even came to work for the Christian Appalachian Project.[2]

It was also in 1981 that Bishop Hughes asked Father Beiting to take over a mission parish in the Big Sandy area of Eastern Kentucky, covering Floyd and Magoffin Counties. He was surprised, but agreed to accept this new assignment. When news reached his parishioners, it almost seemed to be an act of betrayal to move this beloved priest to an area 150 miles away. Even senior citizens of the community organized as a group and wrote to the Bishop, hoping he would reconsider his decision.[3] Beiting was also sad to leave the parish and community, especially those people who stood by him and helped his many causes. They had become family to him.[4]

Beiting's new task called for him to carry on his work in one of the most highly depressed areas of Appalachia. He would serve as pastor in Floyd County, at St. Juliana Church in the town of Martin, and St. Theodore in Prestonsburg, along with starting the first Catholic church in Magoffin County. These places were located in the heart of the coal mining region. At that time, Kentucky produced more coal than any other state in America. Yet, while the industry increased production by fifteen percent in Appalachia during this period, over ten thousand miners lost their jobs. Mechanization, which caused this demise further magnified the unemployment situation in Eastern Kentucky. Coal mining had been the largest employer in the area, and for most people, the only source of income. In places like Mud Creek, Floyd County, up to seventy-five percent of the working population was unemployed because no other industry existed. Overall, a greater percentage of the people in this area lived below the poverty level than in any other part of our nation.[5]

When Beiting first came to the mountains as a seminarian, he witnessed that poverty isolated people in different ways. In the 1980's, the hillfolk were not as much in physical isolation anymore, but had greater spiritual needs. During the late 1940s, twenty-five percent of eastern Kentuckians belonged to an organized religion, while in the 1980s only sixteen percent were members of a church. Many people had lost their faith, or were no longer members of an organized religion and lived life far removed from God. Beiting had to face the question of whether or not the church could survive in this part of Appalachia as an influential force, affecting people's lives. He was not even sure if the people could survive. The economic future looked bleak, and if history repeated itself, Appalachia would lose some of the most vital and energetic persons through out-migration. Eventually, the churches lost not only members, but individuals with leadership qualities.[6]

At the same time, several denominations were going through a period of philosophical differences, causing frustration for many people. The major conflict was no longer between Catholic and Protestant churches, but surfaced among mainline Protestants and Fundamentalists. "As is the case in every religious war, it is the church itself that suffers most," Beiting said. It saddened him, for his ecumenical work had made great strides toward bringing the religions of Appalachia together. However, this did not alter his belief that for churches to grow, people had to be tolerant of each other. "This doesn't mean we give up our principles, but that we give up our judgments of each other," he said. "Let God be the judge."[7]

In extending his hand to clergy of all religions, he urged them to deal with the plight of the unchurched people.

There is no such thing as a soul by itself on this earth.
We bring body and soul with us always. All churches
must accept and serve both if we are to be God's voice
in the wilderness. The church must turn more and
more to the non-churched. We need to stop raiding
one another's sheep and seek out those who have
no shepherd.[8]

Probably the greatest change during this period was the growth of the electronic church. The rise of televangelism in the late 1970s and early 1980s led to a decline of worshippers at local churches. People seemed to be content to stay at home, watching and listening to a nationally known preacher, rather than attend a place of worship. Choirs on television were magnificent, and the floral arrangements of one program alone cost more than a small congregation could afford in a year. Many of the electronic religious programs had a twenty-four hour prayer line and solicitation, and the local pastor found it difficult to compete. Thus, the 1980s saw church attendance decreasing, while the audience of televangelism grew each week.[9]

As the electronic programs mushroomed and certain evangelists were raising unbelievable sums of money—in one case $128 million a year—the religious dollar became limited for local churches. However, the televangelist scandals of the last half of the 1980s led to decreased contributions and people questioned all religious groups and Christian charities. Many wanted more accountability of their donations. Local churches such as Father Beiting's and charities, like the Christian Appalachian Project, were able to provide that.

Beiting continued within his new parish to offer outreach programs and align with community issues for the social good of all people. With optimism, he felt that his parishioners would give to these causes. He emphasized the Biblical concept of stewardship by stressing the need to donate "time, treasures, and talents." Involvement by his parishioners was evident as they contributed not only to their church, but to the community as well.[10]

When Bishop Hughes transferred Father Beiting to Floyd County, the move caused concern among CAP's staff. However, Beiting assured them that his role as president would continue, and he had no intention of abandoning the organization. In fact, he began to plan for expansion of the overall operation and studied new territories, thinking of the best way for CAP to make a contribution to Floyd and Magoffin counties.

Beiting told his staff that he wanted the Lancaster operations center kept intact. Aware of the importance of stability in the organization, he expressed his confidence in the leadership of the administrative staff. As a close knit group, they would carry on in an effective manner with the daily operation. At the time Beiting founded CAP, he knew eventually other challenges would confront him, and when that day came he made sure that everything was in place for a smooth transition.

Beiting faced his new situation humbly and head on, still running the Christian Appalachian Project from 150 miles away. This called for a demanding and grueling work schedule. He said Mass every day at St. Juliana Church in Martin, met new parishioners and ministered to their needs. At Prestonsburg, he negotiated a trade for a former Baptist church, located on the outskirts near Jenny Wiley State Park, and remodeled it for Catholic worship in that part of Floyd County. In Magoffin County, he bought property and a trailer, which was used as a chapel to accommodate the people in Salyersville.[11]

On top of this, Father Beiting skillfully steered CAP toward a program of expansion, and recruited Mike Sanders as the first full-time employee for the Floyd-Magoffin area. A Pike County native, Sanders' military duties had taken him to Texas, where he married Jackie Taylor. After his honorable discharge from the U.S. Armed Forces, Mike worked in Texas for a few years, then returned to Prestonsburg and opened a service station. Through his wife, a parishioner of the Catholic church in Floyd County, Mike met Father Beiting. Their relationship had started on a business level and quickly grew into a personal friendship. Rather than accept a lucrative position in mining, Sanders joined CAP for a significantly less income, because Beiting's work and the organization impressed him. Mike had never considered a career in service work, "but answered the call to help change the quality of life in Floyd County."[12]

"During my beginning years, there was never a boring moment working with Father Beiting," Sanders recalls. "At the same time that programs started, new ones were ready to jump into action. We were always on the go, looking for something new to start, or trying to help someone. It's just completely different from anything else I've ever done, and very exciting."[13] As director of CAP's operations in the area, Mike gave stability to the fledgling programs. Because he grew up in Eastern Kentucky, his insights were invaluable, and his presence provided credibility to the organization.

Also in the 1980s, Father Beiting continued to street preach several weeks each summer throughout Appalachia. This type of evangelization was a challenge that appealed to his desire to comfort those who needed enrichment of spirituality. "I could see the effect street preaching had on the people," Beiting said. "I think many Christians forgot that Christ said, 'Go forth and preach the Gospel.' "[14] This face-to-face approach of taking God's Word to the people as Jesus did, continued to be an imposing force for his ministry.

During this time, Father Beiting expanded his evangelization to include other priests and ministers, along with the Mountain Troubadors, a group of gospel singers recruited from the CAP volunteer program. Traveling to many of these communities over the years, he had built strong relationships with families. People remembered him preaching and looked forward to his return because he had a special way of communicating God's love to them. Beiting would always emphasize Christian unity and the importance of family, and after preaching, he walked among the people, thanked them for listening, and talked about their questions and problems. Many times, this missionary activity was indispensable to those who had lost a living sense of the faith.

On one occasion, a woman was touched to hear his message about the importance of the family. Father Beiting saw that she was carrying a heavy burden, and asked if they could talk. He found out that the woman's husband had left her and their three children. For a while, she lived with her mother, who eventually threw this confused, shattered person and her young ones out of the house. These experiences, along with feeling a lack of purpose in her life, resulted in a breakdown and loss of self-esteem. She and her children then moved into a log cabin, where intolerable living conditions existed. Her situation became so intractable that she found herself in a mental and physical stranglehold. Unhappiness mounted, even though she later moved into a housing project. She had lost hope and became indifferent to her friends' encouragement to believe in God. During their discussion Father Beiting motivated this woman to renew her faith in the Lord. She realized that her outlook on life had to change, and she was ready to move on, as a new self-awareness and spiritual uplift had embodied her.[15]

In February of 1982, Beiting learned from Bishop Hughes

Father Beiting welcomes Mother Teresa and her missionaries of Charity to Jenkins, Kentucky on June 19, 1982.

that members of Mother Teresa's order, the Missionaries of Charity, wanted to establish a community in Appalachia to serve the poor. This was significant, for it brought attention to the

American people of the increased awareness that religious organizations were having about the plight of Appalachia's society. At that time, over forty religious communities of men and women had representatives in the Covington Diocese mountain region.[16]

During the first week of March, Beiting took Bishop Hughes and his assistant, Father Raymond Hartman, along with Sister Priscilla Lewis of Mother Teresa's order, to tour Appalachia and select a location for their work. After considerable travel throughout the region, Sister Priscilla made her decision and Father Beiting helped the sisters acquire a house in Jenkins, Kentucky. He volunteered CAP workers to remodel the home, and on May 30, four nuns moved into the renovated residence-chapel facility. Knowing they were without transportation, Beiting donated a used station wagon for the sisters.[17]

Mother Teresa, who came to visit the sisters, dedicated the facility on June 19 and 20, 1982. Although there were very few Catholics in Jenkins, the entire population welcomed Mother Teresa to their community. Jenkins overflowed with visitors that weekend, and some had traveled from as far away as Massachusetts. "There was great excitement that this world renowned religious group and its revered leader had risen to the challenge of helping the poor in the Jenkins area," Father Beiting said. "I think it's a tribute to their wisdom that they chose Appalachia to begin their rural work in the United States." Since their arrival, the sisters have responded to people on a daily basis, while CAP provided them with donated food, goods, supplies, clothing, furniture and appliances for distribution to the needy.

Shortly after arriving in the Floyd-Magoffin area, Father Beiting noted that a significant percentage of youngsters did not finish high school. "Many were removed from the outside world because they felt inadequate to compete. They just were not eager to get excited about the future," he said. "They lacked confidence to rise beyond the level they were at." In addition, most of the educational systems had limited resources to help those students with the greatest needs. Beiting knew that youngsters who came from caring families had a chance of making it in Eastern Kentucky, as well as anywhere else. However, he was disheartened by the frustration of those whose future looked dim and directionless. He explains:

> *For the student whose parents aren't involved, or maybe don't appreciate the value of education, that child is condemned to a loneliness in which he or she is not going to be able to grow beyond what it feels, touches, or sees. They can't imagine; their perception is limited; they live in a prison—and that's poverty.*[18]

This was not new to Father Beiting, because it reminded him of what he had seen when he first came to Appalachia in the fifties. He recalls that the lack of education and absence of motivation in the hill country had been constant for generations. "It was a major theme back in the early 1900s when Alice Lloyd and the Settlement schools came to Eastern Kentucky to begin their movement to help educate the people."[19] Back then, physical isolation was a major deterrent for children to attend school, because roads and transportation were lacking. However, in the 1980s, youngsters had the opportunity of being bused to school. Yet, Beiting saw that spiritual isolation was still a major deterrent, and decided to take action to improve the situation.

To bring about change for the children of this area, Father

Beiting expressed his desire to start an interdenominational school in Floyd County. This ecumenical idea was well received at a meeting of citizens on August 20, 1982, in Martin, Kentucky. Thirty-nine people of various denominations met to discuss Beiting's proposal for a Christian school.[20]

With great enthusiasm, they gave unanimous approval for a school dedicated to excellence and the spirit of God. Thus, the Mountain Christian Academy came into existence. Beiting's intent was to create a unique comprehensive educational community consisting of five distinct learning programs: a child development center for three, four and five year olds; a grade school; four years of high school; an evening GED program; and an adult learning center offering college and enrichment courses. He also envisioned interdenominational cooperation as the basis for easing existing religious tensions. Beiting felt that involving all faiths and allowing each denomination to gather its members for religious instructions during the first period of the school day would prove to be a powerful force for excellence in learning, and spiritual growth. He further encouraged family involvement as another dimension of the school's special character. Parents were asked to contribute to the learning process at school as well as committing themselves to study time at home with their children.[21]

In July of 1983, Marilyn Stefanski moved from Lancaster to Martin to plan the child development day care program for children ages three to five. Benedictine Sister Judy Yunker became Dean of the Academy, and coordinated with Stefanski the curriculum planning and scheduling activities for the September 12, 1983 opening. From the beginning, The Mountain Christian Academy dedicated itself to bring together students of different social and economic backgrounds. Scholarships were given to youngsters who came from families that lived in poverty. Father Beiting felt that by mixing students from poor and well-to-do families, would create a healthy learning environment filled with Christian spirit. Even though it may have been difficult and unrealistic for most Appalachian schools at this time to motivate children to learn, many Mountain Christian Academy students excelled academically, and were able to move on to institutions of higher education.

With the expansion of CAP services and programs, it became increasingly clear to Beiting that the income for running the total operation was not sufficient. In addition, money was needed for the development of new CAP initiatives and activities. Adding staff and facilities, as well as providing housing for more volunteers, were also necessary ingredients for the organization's continued growth.

The volunteer program grew to fifty men and women who committed themselves to serve for a year or more, mainly in outreach and educational work. In addition, approximately 1500 part-time volunteers came every year to help for a week to six months. CAP also employed over two hundred people full-time, and another two hundred for seasonal and part-time jobs. Besides human development programs, employees participated in service and administrative functions that were needed to support CAP's work throughout Appalachia.[22]

This expansion was not without consequence, and Father Beiting's tried-and-true method of raising money through direct mail became a major concern during that decade. A self-assessment of the organization in 1982 showed that there would be a gross deficiency in available monies to help meet the increase of programs and services. In previous years, added income generally insured steady growth. However, the 1980s saw CAP take a more challenging and dynamic approach to widening its scope of operation by providing for a greater number of needy citizens. As a result, the organization's budget multiplied extensively.

Realizing the implications of the budget increase, Father Beiting took aggressive action. He established new methods of fund raising that included planned giving, as well as solicitation from foundations, corporations, and church congregations. However, CAP did not solicit solely monetary support, but also included requests for volunteers, materials, supplies, food, goods, other in-kind gifts, and prayer. With the dissemination of information telling of the problems in Appalachia, Beiting's campaign faced greater challenges, and he had to inspire many more individuals and organizations to respond to his call.[23]

Shortly after his transfer to Floyd-Magoffin counties in November of 1982, he restructured CAP's leadership into a management team and left the daily operations in the hands of Mike McLaughlin, Bill Begley, Ellen Burke, Moe Mercier, Bill Watson and Ed Wardle. Mike Sanders would join them later. Implementing the management team freed Father Beiting to concentrate on raising funds.[24]

As he started his fund raising campaign during the early part of the eighties, Beiting found that non-profit religious organizations, colleges, universities, and televangelists were in fierce competition for money. This led him to expand his work to include television and radio presentations, lecturing before a variety of groups and organizations, and even visiting the homes of philanthropists. He gave sermons in churches of every denomination on the need to give. This became a major undertaking because of the fact that stewardship of people giving their time, talents, and treasures, was a relatively new approach to many churchgoers. When people said they couldn't afford to give, he told them that their contributions would truly make a difference, regardless of how little they gave. Beiting further explained that generosity was two-fold. "First, there are the material things that people give, but beyond that is the love which prompts them to make a contribution. God uses that love in a marvelous way to bring about change. Charity conveys an on-going love, which makes people think of others more than themselves and, at the same time, is rewarding."[25]

On April 14, 1984, Father Beiting's mother, Martha, passed away at the age of eighty-two, after a struggle with cancer. Survivors included her husband, Ralph T. Beiting, seven sons and four daughters, forty-six grandchildren, and thirty-five great-grandchildren. In his eulogy, Father Beiting said to the mourners with emotion in his voice, "Many of you know that first and foremost, my mother was a lover of life. She loved her husband, children, grandchildren, neighbors, and throughout life she demonstrated her love in simple, yet important ways."[26]

There was so much he did not say, but afterward, Father Beiting remembered that a startling thing happened at the time of her death. "She was in such excruciating pain from bone cancer that the nurses kept saying to her, 'Mrs. Beiting, why don't you scream or yell to relieve the pain?.' She looked at them and simply said, 'No, I can offer it for my son and the work that goes on in the mountains. I can help the people through my suffering to ask God's blessing upon them.'" Father Beiting also remembered, "Just days before her death, she instructed my sisters to get all of her belongings and whatever there was of value and put on a yard sale. She wanted the proceeds to go to the missions in the mountains."[27] Mrs. Beiting died one day after all the items were sold.

During the period of mourning, Father Beiting's friends, parishioners, fellow workers and volunteers were very supportive. Keeping himself busy and praying daily for his mother helped strengthen his resolve, even though heartache prevailed.

It became difficult for him and his family to get through the holidays, for things were not the same anymore. Knowing that his parishioners and CAP needed him, Beiting worked through his feelings of sadness, and involved himself more deeply in his activities.

As CAP began to grow in the coal-producing region of Eastern Kentucky, Father Beiting's example became a stronger inspiration each day for the local people. Volunteers from Floyd, Magoffin, Knott, Pike, Perry, Breathitt, and Letcher counties joined CAP workers to make their presence known to the poor people. He saw in these concerned citizens sincerity and commitment to help make Appalachia a better place to live. Most of them had grown up in Eastern Kentucky and understood the conditions of poverty, and by working with CAP, they were part of a crusade to bring change to the area. Many needy people, ingrained with poor living habits and attitudes of defeatism, were enlightened with dignity by CAP workers and volunteers on how to help themselves. With Mike Sanders at the helm, Beiting was able to create cohesiveness in developing successful programs and services.[28]

In the mid 1980s, Father Beiting established new initiatives for families. During these years, the Appalachian family experienced increased social problems. Floyd-Magoffin, and surrounding counties were in dire need for all types of assistance. In meeting CAP's philosophy of emphasizing the total family, programs and services were expanded to include the Big Sandy area, touching thousands of families each year.

Like Cliffview and Camp Andrew Jackson, which were established in the fifties and sixties, Father Beiting felt that similar types of facilities for children in the Big Sandy area would be one way to involve the family. Since Floyd County was home to Dewey Lake and its many potentialities, he explored the area.

Within a short time, CAP built two new camps. The first year, summer camp was held at Camp Rebecca Boone, a remote lakeside area located a few miles from the main dock on Dewey Lake. The only way to get to this camp was by boat. The following year, the Christian Appalachian Project acquired Camp Shawnee through an arrangement with the Boy Scouts of America and the U.S. Army Corps of Engineers. For years, the Boy Scouts had leased this 300-acre tract of land from the Corps. When it fell into disrepair, CAP negotiated to take over the lease.[29]

Immediately CAP workers and volunteers constructed new buildings, playing fields for baseball, soccer, and football, and built a pool, along with installing a major dock. Camp Shawnee became a beautiful place, filled with an abundance of activities. Each summer, over eight hundred children came to camp, with approximately half of them returning from previous years. Activities involved a thirty-eight mile boat trip on the lake, and a night outing to dramatic productions at Jenny Wiley Summer Music Theater. Also, several specialized camps were sponsored by CAP each summer, including a computer workshop that operated in conjunction with Berea College.

Most children who attended camp were very poor, and had never thought of having the opportunity to enjoy a healthy and happy summer experience. Father Beiting saw new challenges for their growth by integrating disadvantaged and well-to-do youngsters. Like the Mountain Christian Academy, he felt that summer camp was a good tool to bring all social classes together, and in spite of criticism, many people agreed with his rationale for wanting to do this.

We can encourage children to be open to new ideas
and gain greater confidence. We can help bring hope

*into their lives and a sense of partnership with the
outside world. We can influence them. Yet, we need
to take care of the poor and get the whole community involved. If the people don't associate with the
poor, they're certainly not going to have an idea of
the difficulties presented to a family. We'll never solve
Appalachia's problems unless we make the people
aware of them.*[30]

During the eighties, the increase in family violence led Father Beiting to evaluate the situation at hand. Even though CAP
had spousal abuse centers in Mt. Vernon and Somerset, the Big
Sandy area was lacking in this type of service, and many victims had nowhere to turn to for help. Beiting saw the need for
action, and with assistance of his workers, he developed the
Big Sandy Family Abuse Center that would serve Floyd, Johnson,
Martin, Magoffin, and Pike counties.[31]

While the Big Sandy Center services were targeted toward
victims, perpetrators also received help in family and group
counseling, if they were willing. The staff educated communities about domestic violence, and established a twenty-four
hour crisis hotline to assist victims before and after they came
to the shelter. In addition, CAP sponsored conferences that fea-
tured Christian speakers, medical and legal professionals, as
well as family and marriage counselors who provided their
expertise. Included in this comprehensive approach to battle
domestic violence were classes and discussion groups for individuals and couples, as well as the total family.

As Father Beiting continued to help create change in Appalachia, he brought together a core of Kentucky's leaders and
citizens to share thoughts, ideas, and concerns about the future. He hoped that the results would lead to a difference in

the lives of the region's people. In June of 1985, CAP sponsored a two-day symposium at Berea College, which was called, "Appalachia: A Vision for Action." Among the issues discussed was the quality of health care in Eastern Kentucky, because Beiting felt that for too long very little had been done in this field. Soon afterward, he held a preventive health care meeting, which marked the beginning of a cooperative venture between CAP and Eastern Kentucky University, specifically with Dr. Oris Blackwell, Chairman of the Environmental Health Department.[32]

CAP focused on developing a staff to coordinate this venture which was first known as "Preventive Health," and later changed to the Community Health Advocates Program (CHAP). The original staff were Suzie Smith, from California, and Sue McDuffy and Jean Kowalski, both of Wisconsin, all registered nurses. They began researching living conditions, including drinking water, methods of waste disposal, household heating, and the occurrence of recent chronic illnesses within a targeted area known as Arkansas Creek. The nurses then took their results and began designing initiatives to educate people living in the Arkansas Creek area and surrounding communities about the importance of sanitary water.[33]

Since those beginning days, the CHAP staff has gone on to work in schools, youth and senior citizen centers, and homes. As its service area grew, the program remained constant in helping people to help themselves by teaching them about healthy choices and lifestyles.

In the 1980s, illiteracy continued to be a major obstacle for many people in almost every area of Appalachia. Beiting knew that before these individuals could get their high school diploma, they had to have the most basic skills, including reading and writing. The urgency to educate the high percentage of non-readers led the Christian Appalachian Project to develop courses and cooperative ventures with local learning centers and schools that offered classes for adults. During the early stages of this program, Beiting expressed concern that CAP had been reaching only a few people. He initiated a new approach to improve services, which meant that his teachers had to go out to the backcountry hollows, since those were the greatest areas of need. This homebound approach was especially valuable for mothers with small children, the elderly, and handicapped persons. "It was exciting to see that people no longer had to go to the school in town," he recalled. Instead, CAP workers and volunteers were traveling to work with them at home."[34]

As response from the people grew, CAP found it more difficult for teachers to cover the area. A worker came up with the idea that they could provide better service by using a mobile classroom. Employees from the adult education, home repair, and vehicle maintenance programs teamed up to convert an old school bus into a classroom. They dismantled seats, and installed desks and tables. Workers added a rest room, and a generator provided electricity for typewriters, calculators, and computers. Thus, the "Little Red School Bus" started its successful journey as CAP personnel tutored teenagers and adults, who were working on high school equivalency certificates (GED) and literacy instruction. As this unique educational approach proved to be effective by serving more people each year, a private foundation donated funding to renovate a second bus. The success of the "Little Red School Bus" program was so outstanding that it gained attention of the national media. A feature article with pictures appeared in the National Geographic Magazine, and CNN provided television coverage of this venture.[35]

Since the beginning of Father Beiting's ministry, gifts-in-kind have comprised a major part of donations to the Christian Appalachian Project. In the beginning of 1986, a significant in-kind gift led to a new service by CAP. Bill Begley, now Vice President of Development, received a telephone call from an acquaintance in Virginia, who asked if CAP had interest in children's books. Begley gave an affirmative response, but did not anticipate the overwhelming donation. When he traveled to Virginia to arrange transportation, he was faced with twenty-four tractor-trailers loaded with books. CAP warehouses could not accommodate this enormous contribution. Congressman Hal Rogers, of Kentucky, was made aware of the situation, and contacted Bill Newell, who owned a large tobacco warehouse in Somerset, Kentucky, about CAP's need for storage space. Newell offered the use of his warehouse, but the books had to be out by the beginning of the tobacco season. Christian Appalachian Project programs used as many books as they could, and distributed the rest to non-profit organizations in Kentucky, West Virginia, Alabama, North Carolina, Ohio, Virginia and Tennessee.[36]

With the addition of storage space and starting a multi-state network, CAP hired a local man named Charlie Deaton to manage the donation of books and their distribution. CAP would also play a more significant role in the Appalachian mountain range states through the work of this new program which was named Operation Sharing.

Since a system for distribution of donations was established, Beiting's workers continued to contact companies to provide all types of surplus goods for Appalachia's needy. By the end of 1986, CAP's staff had solicited support from corporations, organizations, and individuals throughout the country. As a result, Operation Sharing was able to touch approximately

400,000 people in the previously mentioned Appalachian states, through the distribution of such items as books, garden seeds, toys, food, and clothing.

Father Beiting expressed enthusiasm about the impact that Operation Sharing created. He asked his staff to draw up long range plans for the program. The guidelines for eligible organizations to receive goods from Operation Sharing were developed to make sure that materials reached persons of need as gifts-in-kind, and not to be sold.

Furthermore, Beiting felt that for Operation Sharing to accomplish its goals, the Christian Appalachian Project should play a supporting role to other charitable organizations. The motivating force behind this belief was that sharing with church groups and non-profit agencies would provide the best direct service to those in need. "There was no better way of knowing the needs of people than the local church or agency," he said.[37] Because of CAP's contribution during this time, Appalachia also saw the formation of these charitable organizations pursue their goals with greater community involvement. Many would not have been as effective without the support of Operation Sharing. Even though CAP had already established a nucleus of groups and agencies to work with, this was far from meeting Father Beiting's goal for the future.

1986 was the start of a hectic period of growth, as the Christian Appalachian Project built warehouses, rented buildings, bought trucks, and hired personnel to take in all the donations. Every year thereafter, contributions increased as trucks unloaded daily throughout Appalachia. In Lancaster, Tyner, and Hagerhill, workers and volunteers sorted, stored, and then distributed the goods. By the end of the eighties, churches, charities, social agencies, and community groups throughout the thirteen state Appalachian region and beyond received these goods from Operation Sharing that benefited hundreds of thousands of people annually.[38]

At the same time Operation Sharing was getting underway, Bishop William Hughes met with Father Beiting to discuss plans of a new assignment to raise funds for the Diocese's missions. The bishop knew that Father Beiting's fund raising approach was successful, and his knowledge and expertise to convey the extremes and needs of the mountain people produced excellent results.

Before embarking on his new assignment, the transitional period was not only important for Beiting, but for the Christian Appalachian Project personnel as well. Even though he would continue his fund raising efforts for CAP and stay on as Chairman of the Board, Father Beiting relinquished his presidency, and appointed Mike McLaughlin to that position. During the transition, Beiting kept a watchful eye on things, for he wanted the administrative staff to feel secure in the day-to-day operation of the organization. His desk always seemed loaded with papers, many relating to new initiatives, services, or programs. It was a hectic time, and catching up on unfinished business seemed endless, and as he approached the day of his new assignment, he was confident that the organization would carry on in an effective manner.[39]

On July 1, 1986, Beiting assumed duties as associate to Father Thomas Mittendorf, Director of the Diocesan Mission Office. Responding to Beiting's request that his home-base be located in Appalachia, Bishop Hughes also assigned him to serve as part-time chaplain to the Benedictine Sisters at the Dwelling Place Monastery in Mount Tabor, Floyd County. As a result, CAP and diocesan workers built a small office-residence on the monastery grounds for him.[40] His first task for the Diocesan Mission Office was to institute a Speakers Network that included twenty-eight sisters, fifteen priests, and six lay persons. They traveled throughout the United States and made presentations to various groups about the needs of Appalachia, in hopes of raising money, interest, and volunteerism.[41]

Beiting played an important part in gaining greater support for the missions from other dioceses. Over the next two years, twenty-three dioceses in the United States would have mission offices actively involved with the Appalachian region. Through his efforts to educate directors of these offices about the importance of their involvement, an effective organized support system was developed.

During this time, the televangelist scandals were creating negative attitudes among citizens toward religious organizations. Fund raising became a major concern, as people no longer gave generously. They also wanted to know how their contributions were used. Thousands of persons heard Father Beiting talk, and knew that his work was sincere and accountable. Touching the hearts of his listeners, he explained in a simple and humble way why he needed their help. He laid a solid foundation of teaching them the theology of giving and its spiritual benefits.

Beiting's talks did not lead to brief spurts of support but proved to be the beginning of lifelong habits of stewardship, where people donated through prayer, faith, and sacrifice.

> *I personally don't conceive of it as fund raising, because I really don't like raising funds. I know that you only get money when people are motivated. You can't take it away from them. You really need to be able to sell this to people. So, I look upon my job as selling the excitement of God. I look at my task as trying to be a herald for that kind of challenge.*[42]

During November of 1986, Father Beiting went to Africa at the request of the Catholic Relief Services (CRS) on a fact-finding mission. He heard stories of how relief shipments sent to Ethiopia and other developing nations became spoiled and useless on the docks. Also, rumors had it that government officials pilfered supplies for their own political ends. [43]

In his travel throughout Ethiopia, Senegal, and Mauritania, Beiting did not find the wasteful, bungled relief effort that he had heard about. Instead, he observed an established network of approximately five hundred Catholic Relief Service workers operating a truck fleet that outperformed the United Nations in its effectiveness to reach the starving. The Catholic Relief Services had strategically built warehouses and distribution centers so effectively that they were reaching the most remote villages in these countries.

The methods Father Beiting saw were modeled from those he had developed in Appalachia. The Catholic Relief Services approach focused on discouraging people from becoming totally dependent, even though they would not refuse aid to those in need. For example, if a man received a substantial food allotment, he contributed his labor for several days. He might assist by planting trees on deforested land, or irrigating fields in the fight against drought. Beiting observed that projects built on established resources created a sense of community, as the people were provided with incentives to become self-dependent.

Similarities in method between Catholic Relief Services and the Christian Appalachian Project may not have been totally coincidental. Ken Curtin, who organized the Catholic Relief Services fact-finding mission, served as one of Father Beiting's volunteers during the 1970s. "I find it fascinating to see how effective his approach had become," Curtin said.[44]

Later, Beiting explained how there was no way to brace himself for some of the things he witnessed. Tent cities of refugees, orphanages with hundreds of hungry children, and crude clinics that lacked the essentials and staff to treat tuberculosis, malaria, and leprosy, exposed the reality of human suffering in Africa. Yet, Father Beiting had seldom seen so much compassion at work. The giving of the religious and lay workers continued twenty-four hours a day, seven days a week. "I have never been so proud of Christianity," he said. "It was in action, and not empty talk, rationalizing, or philosophizing. It was not getting lost in agencies, but people helping their brothers and sisters."

Every summer, since he arrived in Appalachia, Father Beiting took to the back country to street preach. However, in 1987, he came up with the idea of preaching from a houseboat.[45] For two weeks in June of that year, he and his entourage set out on the Kentucky and Ohio Rivers for a five hundred and twenty-mile "water borne" preaching tour, covering twelve ports in four states. Traveling on the flag-bedecked *Daniel Boone*, Beiting was joined by fellow preachers and old friends, including Reverend Doyle Fortney, a Church of God minister from Louisville, Kentucky, and Father Frank Osburg, pastor of St. Michael's Parish in Paintsville, Kentucky. Reverend Fortney had served as director of personnel and spiritual programs for CAP. Father Osburg, was a former associate pastor to Father Beiting during his first years in the mountains. They were also joined by an Episcopal priest, Father Joe Hannon, at Maysville, Kentucky. Bowden Atherton, a minister from Tulsa, Oklahoma, met the group in Cincinnati. Reverend Walter Hill, pastor of the Parkland Church of God in Louisville, and Larry Jones of "Feed the Children" organization and a minister from Oklahoma City, came on board at New Albany, Indiana. Lynne Blankenship,

As part of his outreach ministry, Beiting street preaches every summer.

manager of CAP's volunteer program and a Methodist minister, joined the preachers on the last quarter of the trip. "We
wanted to demonstrate that we could live, pray, and preach
together as friends," said Beiting. A group of CAP volunteers
served as crew, provided maintenance for the sixty-eight foot
boat, and performed as the Mountain Troubadors at each stop.

Along with his desire to preach the gospel, Beiting's intent
was to make others aware of the hardships in Appalachia. He
wanted to bond the people of the mountain region with those
of middle-America. "Unless we are together in love, we are not
together in God. We need to work and pray together to have
Him in our midst," Father Beiting said. "We have to bring God
out of the churches and into the world where we work and
play so that we, through Him, can make a difference."[46]

During each stop, the preachers recounted stories from
Scriptures and experiences that illustrated how individuals

found hope through faith in God, and His love and concern for the people. As the priests and ministers addressed the audiences on the banks of the river at Portsmouth and Cincinnati, television crews came on board to tape parts of the gospel tour. CBS's *Sunday Morning* with Charles Kurault, and *Reel to Real* a syndicated TV program, joined the parade of media who followed along. The tour also drew attention from newspapers and magazines with interviews given at all ports.[47]

Father Beiting hoped the tour would inspire people "to look at their lives differently, and have a change of mind, attitude and heart." The excellent attendance was an indication that they came to listen because of their faith in his mission.

In the beginning of 1988, the Apostolic Delegate in Washington, D.C., Archbishop Pio Laghi, had been meeting with the bishops of the province that included Tennessee and Kentucky, relating to restructuring certain dioceses. One of their recommendations was to separate the mountain region from the Covington Diocese and combine it with seven Appalachian counties that originally were part of the Louisville jurisdiction. Beiting had also written to the archbishop, supporting the formation of a new diocese.[48]

With the pope's approval to establish the Diocese of Lexington, Archbishop Laghi contacted Father Beiting and asked his opinion about potential candidates for the position of bishop. Beiting responded by recommending Auxiliary Bishop J. Kendrick Williams of the Covington Diocese, whose friendship he treasured. "He has had a strong concern for the mountain region, and I hope he will have many years to exercise his leadership," Beiting said. "I believe he is a genuinely concerned individual and one with deep feelings for all those who are doing the work of God."[49]

The day Williams became bishop of the new Diocese of Lexington, he had been visiting with Beiting at Mount Tabor, and talking to CAP volunteers who were interested in religious life. It was not until the next morning that he learned of his appointment. Beiting knew that Bishop Williams would gain strong support from the priests in the diocese. His ideas for a progressive approach to assisting the mountain parishes were important to Appalachia. Also, his active participation and leadership would increase the effectiveness of the church in meeting the needs of more people.

At this time, Father Beiting faced an important decision regarding his own future. Even though his work as fund-raiser for the Covington Diocese missions was successful, he wanted to stay and serve the mountain people through the newly formed Diocese of Lexington. Consequently, Bishop Williams asked him to continue as fundraiser and work part-time as chaplain at Mount Tabor in Floyd County.[50]

On June 9, 1988, Ralph T. Beiting passed away at the age of 87. Following a funeral Mass at St. Joseph Church in Cold Springs, Kentucky, Mr. Beiting was entombed at St. Stephen Mausoleum, Ft. Thomas, next to his wife Martha. Gifted by God, he was a man of strong character and determination, who rose from poverty to become successful in the construction field, and served as a union leader, as well as Mayor of Highland Heights, Kentucky.[51] As one dear friend said after the funeral, "What an impact his life has had on earth." He and his wife, Martha, were CAP's first volunteers, and with their children, they became the Christian Appalachian Project's strongest supporters.[52]

Among the people nurtured by this family was Kathleen Ford Leavell, a friend and dedicated CAP worker for many years. She wrote of Mr. Beiting,

Over the past several weeks, as my thoughts have turned to the impact of his life on all of us, I became more and more aware of how many wonderful things were rooted in the love of Ralph T. Beiting and his beautiful wife, Martha. Had they not chosen to teach their children how to love God and reflect this love in their work for others, many of our lives would be different. When their son formed the Christian Appalachian Project, we found ourselves over the years, a part of this life. We were gifted not only with CAP, but with each other. By becoming family and sharing this faith, hope, love, and hard work, we developed deep and lasting friendships, many of which grew into love and marriage.[53]

There were many good memories of Mr. Beiting, some of which brought smiles to people's faces who knew him well. Kathleen Leavell remembers: "We would take particular pleasure in watching him direct his son in loading or unloading a trailer. It was amusing to see Father Beiting being bossed around. We were touched by the respect and reverence of a great man toward his father."[54]

A few months later, CAP donated Cliffview Lodge to the Diocese of Lexington as a retreat center, in honor of Father Beiting's family, especially his late mother and father. This gift was the first piece of property Beiting had bought in 1957 for his work with the needy people of Appalachia.[55]

During the late 1980s, he took an active role in bringing together the state's leading politicians, professionals, businessmen, and private citizens. Regardless of their political affiliation, they developed a common bond by cooperatively exploring possible economic and social development opportunities.

Participating in different conferences throughout Kentucky and other Appalachian states, Father Beiting also campaigned vigorously for improving economic and social progress through strategies that combined efforts of grass-roots organizations and government agencies.[56]

Given the circumstances, his conviction and dedication to pursuing goals with greater community involvement took a new direction toward having CAP play a leadership role in economic development. For a short time, CAP operated a program that helped communities create economic opportunities by giving technical advice to existing organizations and providing small grants to local groups. The significance of this program did not come about until a few years later, when CAP would implement new economic initiatives with broader ramifications.

In early 1989, Bishop Williams asked Father Beiting if he would undertake a temporary assignment as pastor of St. Michael Church in Paintsville, as a result of the illness of Father Frank Osburg. Previously, Beiting had expressed to the bishop his desire to return to parish work, even though he enjoyed traveling and speaking on behalf of the diocese and CAP. The new assignment was a welcomed challenge since he always had strong feelings for St. Michael Parish and its missions in Lawrence and Martin counties.[57]

In his new assignment, Beiting developed exciting plans for St. Michael Parish. He started by meeting with parishioners and gained an understanding of past directions, ensuring a smooth transition to the future. His goal was not only to serve as spiritual leader, but to help the poor, regardless of their religious background. As in his previous assigned church missions, Beiting's transfer to St. Michael led CAP workers and volunteers to join him in helping the needy of the area. They fed the hungry, nursed the sick, provided clothing and other necessities,

Beiting joins a group of his volunteer singers during one of his annual preaching crusades

and gave counseling to adults and children. Not only did people come to Beiting for help, but he and his followers dedicated their time to visit the needy, whether they lived in towns, small hamlets, or isolated backcountry areas, assisting them in whatever way possible.

In late 1989, the Bluegrass Chapter of the National Conference of Christians and Jews honored Beiting at their Annual Awards Banquet in Lexington, Kentucky, "for outstanding leadership in fostering amity, justice and cooperation among the people..."

When the 1980s came to an end, there were many lingering questions regarding social issues and how to bring about change. Even though Father Beiting's initiatives proved to have a positive affect on people, his longstanding belief of citizen involvement was most crucial for developing solutions to the many ills relating to poverty. He said, "The future of Appalachia lies in the hands of its citizens, no matter how many programs CAP might start. Fostering a sense of community among the people is the foundation from which change will come about. There is no limit to what people can do if they work as a community."[58] Agreeing with this viewpoint, Mike Sanders explained:

> *I think that's why the Christian Appalachian Project has been successful; because the whole CAP family is community. You're not going to find a more spiritual group of people. Everyone cares about each other, or wants to cooperate and help the programs succeed. In this area, it's going to take a real spirit of community. That's one of CAP's strongest points, and something that has to be stressed.*[59]

Sanders further acknowledged that the task ahead would be demanding. "An important lesson one can gain from Father Beiting is that hard work, long hours, and dedication will bring about a better life. To improve the status of living in Appalachia will not be easy, but it most certainly will get better."

However, there were indications that the future was not all bleak. Some progress occurred, despite the continuing battles over issues like education, health care, job opportunities, transportation, and the environment. Even though Beiting and others, who were dedicated to this region, worked hard to create business and industrial initiatives, Appalachians could only detect very little growth to their local economy. As a result, he became more convinced that attracting new business and industry had to come from within Apppalachia and its people. No matter how difficult the task, Father Beiting had great faith that the long pursuit of improving the economic situation would be achievable.

Father Beiting and his friends leading worship on the Danielle Boone at one of many river stops on the Ohio, Kentucky, and Mississippi Rivers.

Courtesy W. Brunner—Berea, Kentucky

Father Beiting and his helpers prepare for a preaching tour on the Ohio River.

Courtesy W. Brunner—Berea, Kentucky

CHAPTER VIII

A Time for Change

In the 1990s more Appalachians than ever before were benefiting from Father Beiting's dynamic leadership. The tradition of addressing the most urgent issues of the time remained his major focus. In addition, CAP not only expanded services to a greater part of the Appalachian range states, but also increased its role with other organizations to help overcome the region's many problems. Consequently, new innovative approaches played an important part in this organization's social programs, and in those with whom it became partners. Economic development in the 1990s witnessed a series of far-reaching changes, as Beiting's earlier ventures gave him an insight and breadth of vision to create new initiatives. Spiritually, his goal was to continue to strengthen and support families.

On January 3, 1990, Father Beiting left Paintsville after saying early morning Mass at St. Michael Church, and drove southwest to Corbin, Kentucky, to visit two struggling companies and see what he could do to help them. Traveling ahead of him in different vans were CAP employees Mike Sanders and Clayton Teel, who accompanied Beiting to these meetings. As he drove along, there was time to reflect and he thought about his brother Ray, who had recently died. He remembered how Ray gave so much of himself by helping to build churches and working on CAP construction projects. Ray had looked forward to coming to Appalachia as a volunteer after his retirement. Unfortunately, he was afflicted with Lou Gehrig's disease and could not fulfill his dreams.

Time passed and Father Beiting was feeling the effects of being overworked. Approaching the outskirts of Hazard, Kentucky, he fell asleep behind the wheel of his van, which smashed into the rear of a tractor-trailer. He was pinned in the vehicle, which caught fire from the tremendous impact. Fortunately, a state trooper and others arrived moments after the accident and extinguished the fire, which required several attempts.[2]

Mike Sanders and Clayton Teel had kept an eye on Father Beiting in their rear view mirrors. When they did not see him for some time, Sanders and Teel turned back and came upon the accident. Father Beiting was conscious and praying. His face had hit the windshield and injuries included head lacerations, a broken jaw and nose, damage to his teeth, a badly mangled leg, and a broken left wrist. Members of the local fire department worked almost two hours to extricate Beiting from his van, and an ambulance took him to the Hazard Regional Hospital, where doctors performed emergency operations. Serious internal injuries were not detected at that time, but complications would lead to later operations. "If there was a time for God to call him home, that was it," Mike Sanders said. "Apparently God felt that his work was not finished on earth."[3]

Father Beiting's recuperation took many months. As word of his accident spread throughout the country many people from all over came to visit him in the hospital as well as in the nursing home, where he completed his recovery. They cared about him and appreciated his many contributions that laid the groundwork for change in the mountain region.

On one occasion, a fellow patient came to see Father Beiting and wished him a speedy recovery. The man mentioned that they had met in his hardware store during the early 1960s in Breathitt County. At that time, certain individuals tried to humiliate Beiting by shouting and throwing things at him while he was street preaching. Even though the storeowner had nothing to do with this group, he apologized for their behavior, and expressed appreciation for Beiting's spiritual, and humanitarian contributions to the area. "As this man stood in my hospital room, it made me feel wonderful to think that he remembered after all these years, and that we had built a bridge between us," Beiting recalls.[4]

On another occasion, a preacher from Topmost in Knott County visited him. A year earlier, Beiting had given him furniture, chairs and desks for the sanctuary and classroom of the local Baptist Church. The preacher was overwhelmed that a Catholic priest would help him and his congregation. "We can't afford to have you die," he said. "What will all the rest of us do if we don't have you here to help and support us, so that we can care for God's people."[5]

These visitors, along with others, reminded Father Beiting how much things had changed since he first came to Appalachia. In his book, *Appalachia...A Special Place...A Bridge of Hope*, Beiting told of the transformation from past days, when he was routinely run off for preaching, threatened with bodily harm, guns, and arrest. He wrote:

> *Bridges made of steel and stone decay and crumble, but the bridges of love and friendship we have built between God's people here in Appalachia grow stronger and stronger with each passing year. Old hatreds are disappearing, and fears are being replaced with*

> *trust and love. Today most of my friends are not*
> *Catholic—something I would never have predicted*
> *forty years ago. Hand-in-hand we are walking to-*
> *ward our heavenly Father across the bridge we have*
> *built together.*[6]

While still in the hospital, Beiting disregarded his doctor's orders to get plenty of rest. He talked with his workers about anything and everything, from donors who wanted to contribute to the organization to initiating economic development projects and jobs. The CAP staff knew that he had to take it easy to fully recover, but as one worker commented, "Beiting always had to be in the thick of activities, directing people through the maze of events and happenings."[7]

As he continued his recovery, the Kentucky House of Representatives passed a resolution applauding Father Beiting for his selfless devotion to the people of Appalachia. At the beginning of March 1990, he checked himself out of the hospital after reconstructive surgery and went back to work in Paintsville. Not very long thereafter, internal complications set in and Beiting was rushed to Kings Daughters Hospital in Ashland, Kentucky, where he had further surgery. After recuperating, he returned to Paintsville at the end of August.

In October, Beiting reported on his health to CAP's Board of Directors, and expressed optimism of returning to work full-time. Mike McLaughlin remembers him saying, "I almost feel that if I can just get through to year's end, my bad luck will all be used up, and you folks might have to put up with me for another ten years at least!" McLaughlin reflected, "It was nice to see he was beginning to feel a few rays of sunshine inside himself, where it counts. That kind of sunshine, enough of it, can make you feel like your cup runneth over. I can't think of anyone who deserved it more."[8]

On December 5, 1990, Beiting received the "National Caring Institute Award" for his devotion to improve the lives of others. The award, given to ten of the most caring persons in the United States, specifically cited that, "Father Beiting has impacted more lives in Appalachia than any other person or organization." In accepting his award, he stated, "I feel deeply about caring. I think it is the only way we can go on and be happy. It is the most instinctive need that any human being has. The world has come to know that caring is the way that happiness comes. I feel privileged to be part of that."[9]

Upon his return to Paintsville on December 7, 1990, Father Beiting was feeling better, even though he had partial sight in one eye, and his injuries were playing havoc with his daily existence. In spite of all this, he started each day with appreciation of being alive, offering Mass, and thanking the Lord for His blessings.

Like most Catholic services, Beiting's were quiet and reverent. However, one Sunday, a three-year old boy escaped from the grasp of his mother, and ran around the church. He was having fun, squealing every time she caught him. Finally, when the worshippers were silently meditating, the child bolted from his mother's arms and ran to the altar, where Father Beiting was sitting. He smiled at the boy and lifted him onto his knee. "The child immediately quieted down, and we sat peacefully for several minutes," Beiting recalls. "On this day, however, I think the whole congregation felt that in this child we had God in our midst. The little boy enjoyed the attention, but not realizing that he was affecting us all. I could sense that he felt safe, bathing in the special kind of love emanating from all the adults surrounding him."

The child stayed with Father Beiting for the remainder of Mass, and they both walked hand-in-hand down the main aisle to the back of the church. After Mass, the child's mother apologized profusely, but Beiting replied, "Please, don't apologize. This was the nicest thing that has happened to me during Mass in a long time."[10]

In April of 1991, Bishop Williams met with Beiting to discuss a new assignment, his fifth in ten years. This was quite a contrast to his first pastoral appointment in Appalachia, which lasted a little over three decades. In this latest move, the bishop asked him to serve as pastor of Lawrence and Martin counties which would be independent from St. Michael's Parish. Father Beiting agreed, and began to plan for a new church in Louisa (Lawrence County). The chapel in Hode (Martin County), consisting of a doublewide trailer, would eventually be transformed into a larger facility.

Even before the move to Louisa in June 1991, Beiting looked for property to build a new church for St. Jude Parish. While the church was under construction, he organized CAP programs. Joining him in August was a group of volunteers, including his assistant, Marilyn Stefanski, and Jim Haragan, who handled the office operation. Vince Turner, who previously worked out of CAP's Mt. Vernon facilities, transferred to Louisa to head the warehouse and distribution center for this area.[11]

As Beiting went into the communities of the area, he was welcomed right away by the people. One local citizen said, "the hillfolk usually don't accept strangers that readily and especially since he was a priest." Yet, Beiting earned immediate respect and support of the people, because he came to help them, and his reputation had preceded him. In viewing the surroundings, he saw conditions of poverty that looked familiar. People's lives were of chronic struggle and uncertainty. With living standards in America having improved through the years, this area was like the rest of Appalachia. It failed to keep up economically, physically, and socially with the rest of the nation. For those who lived in backcountry areas, the many conditions of poverty that previous generations faced, continued into the nineties. Their situations were unbearable as people existed in an isolated environment, where everyone was in need, from the very young to the oldest citizen. The necessities of life for all ages were not being met, which made them more vulnerable to problems of great proportion. They endured life by their own design which was aimed toward continued deteriorating circumstances. Again, Father Beiting was faced with the recurring theme of poverty, and he knew what had to be done.

He immediately purchased a building to store the donations of goods, clothes, furniture, materials, and food, which arrived daily. The facility was then remodeled to include the St. Jude Bargain Outlet, which shared space with the distribution warehouse in Louisa. In Martin County, Beiting bought a facility to develop another bargain store for the needy of that area. Like in other CAP stores volunteers developed relationships with the elderly, adults, children, and disabled and homeless who came in. Services were expanded to include feeding the needy, providing reading classes, counseling, tutoring and emergency assistance.

As programs in Lawrence and Martin counties developed, CAP continued to grow in other areas. In 1991, Father Beiting established the Appalachian Development Corporation (ADC), a for-profit, wholly owned subsidiary of CAP, dedicated to economic improvement of the region. The purpose of ADC was to buy existing businesses or start new ventures, with each employing up to thirty-five people and re-locating them in under-developed areas of Eastern Kentucky.[12] Beiting didn't stop there; he was also concerned with local enterprises that were established, yet needed assistance to help them through hard times.

For instance, during early 1992, he wanted to help a financially strapped friend, who manufactured small fishing and ski boats. Beiting bought these boats and sold them to people for use on the newly developed Yatesville Lake in Lawrence County and other places. This action not only provided a solution to the manufacturer's dilemma, but also kept his workers employed through a tough period. No matter how modestly successful Beiting's initiative appeared to be, it captured the imagination of the people.

The formidable presence of Father Beiting and his organization in Lawrence and Martin counties had brought a spark of light to the poor. Programs were offered for members of poverty-stricken families, which motivated them to take advantage of CAP services. Attracting interdenominational support and local leadership was also an advantage to Beiting's work. Volunteers from the area joined those from outside Appalachia to

Rev. Beiting and his workers distribute goods, food, and clothing to needy families

meet the needs of an expanded base of operation for these two counties. The response from the communities was so overwhelming that CAP services carried over to the West Virginia side of the Big Sandy River.

Since his arrival in this area, Father Beiting gave attention to improving the poor housing conditions. At this time, he inaugurated a spring break Work Fest, hosting approximately four hundred college and university students from all over the United States who painted, built, and repaired houses for low income families, the elderly and the disabled. "The Work Fest was so successful that it became an annual event. Students felt that instead of a few weeks of fun and sun, the hard work to help others was worthwhile and rewarding," Beiting said.[13]

By the end of April 1992, construction of St. Jude Church had progressed, despite problems with materials, contractors, and weather. Father Beiting was determined that the church should be completed for its June dedication. With the addition of new volunteers, he assigned them to work on the church site. On June 28, 1992, Bishop Williams came to Louisa to dedicate St. Jude Church. The residents of this community finally had a place of worship that promoted spiritual growth, and brought together young and old with family-oriented activities.

Immediately thereafter, Father Beiting took to the water to evangelize, as he embarked on a 16-day Appalachian Riverboat Revival tour. He started this trip at Point Pleasant, West Virginia, and traveled 650 miles to Evansville, Indiana. Along with preaching and educating people about the problems in Appalachia, Beiting undertook this journey to celebrate America's sesquicentennial and the 500th anniversary of the introduction of Christianity to the New World.[14]

Before he set out on his river preaching crusade, Father Beiting met with a group of West Virginia ministers in Point

Pleasant, listening to their needs. In the months that followed, his influence became evident. He was able to get the ministerial group a grant to start a food distribution center in West Virginia.[15]

Upon his return to Louisa, Father Beiting was approached by Pathways, a mental health services provider. They were in need of a facility that would accommodate their work with the disabled. Wanting to help them, Beiting acquired property which contained two buildings. Since CAP had need for storage, it would occupy one facility and Pathways the other. With the assistance of temporary volunteers from Ohio, Illinois, and Kansas, CAP workers remodeled the buildings, and Pathways opened its facility in September 1992, to serve families in Lawrence County.[16]

By October 1992, people of the area had built a good relationship with Beiting and CAP. Community support continued to grow when he established a much needed center for young people, literacy classes for adults, and services for the elderly and handicapped. These services and programs provided an important element of support for the recipients to become viable members of the community.

The progress CAP made each day in helping people came about through Father Beiting's ability to recruit dedicated volunteers from all walks of life. For example, Ed Riley, a young man from Massachusetts, traded a well-paid job to contribute his time to the poor. After three years of volunteer service, the inspired Riley entered a seminary outside of Boston. The volunteer ranks also included retired persons, who had deep concerns about Appalachia's poverty. One gentleman, seventy-five year old Larry Dickey, came to CAP from Carmel, California. He had worked in transportation and distribution for the Exxon Corporation, but decided that walking the beach, sitting in the sun, and gardening were not his cup of tea. He still had the energy and desire to contribute to others.[17]

Larry Dickey admitted that one had to consider physical limitations when accepting older people for volunteer service. However, he pointed out that with various types of work, their years of experience could prove to be effective. "To a certain extent, you are a lot more patient with a situation. You can give some support to young volunteers who have never been away from home. Furthermore, it helps to have someone with knowledge of what life is all about, which can be a positive influence on young people with a dream of wanting to help somebody."

On the other hand, it was a young volunteer who inspired George and Margaret Hanafee to work with Father Beiting. Their youngest son had spent a year volunteering in the Dominican Republic. When George retired from work in Detroit, he and his wife felt that to help the poor would be their calling. As a result, their son served as the guiding light in George and Margaret Hanafee's decision to become volunteers with CAP.[18]

The advantages of having older volunteers were many. Not only were they able to share their life experiences, but it also gave them an opportunity to serve as a strong influence on Appalachian youth. "They can do it much the same way that Father Beiting is doing it—by encouraging the kids to stay in school and establish a relationship," George Hanafee said. "Many kids in Kentucky don't have a relationship with their fathers, so they get in trouble or copy people who are not good examples." Whether it was the wisdom of the old or the desire of the young, CAP's volunteers were convinced that Beiting's emphasis of a strong spiritual foundation was necessary for building a solid future.

With the growing number of employees and permanent

volunteers joining Father Beiting, he reached out for new challenges. For instance, one of his major objectives included buying property to expand CAP's operation in Martin County, which was one of the poorest in Appalachia. Beiting knew about an old furniture store and an adjacent house in Inez that would be ideal places for CAP programs and services. He felt that the property could house permanent volunteers, offices for the outreach and elderly visitation programs, an Attic Store, a new chapel, and an activity center. However, he was unable to get monies from CAP due to a tight budget.[19]

Determined to find a way to help the people in Martin County, Father Beiting decided to make a donation of all his personal financial assets. He withdrew his life savings that included a CAP pension and 401K plan through the diocese, and combined it with money borrowed from several friends to buy the property. A diocesan official in charge of contributions remarked, "You should think of yourself and not give all your savings and pension away." Beiting responded, "I am thinking of myself. The only way I can truly be secure is to entrust to God. One must be detached from the material things of our world and show where the real treasure exists." The following year, he donated his tax refund without hesitation to the church.[20]

As Beiting's work became more widely recognized, an honor of great distinction was bestowed upon him and the Christian Appalachian Project. At the 1993 Philanthropy Awards dinner in Atlanta, he accepted the Outstanding Philanthropic Organization of the Year Award from the National Society of Fund Raising Executives. Immediately thereafter, Kentucky Governor Brereton C. Jones responded to the award by writing to Beiting and CAP.[21]

It is with great pride that I congratulate one of Kentucky's assets. Please accept the gratitude of all Kentuckians, especially for the thousands of eastern Kentuckians who are better housed, fed, educated, and qualified for jobs because of your charities.

By the early 1990s, CAP's human development programs had come a long way. A total of seventy direct service projects reached over 100,000 people annually in Eastern Kentucky alone. Programs coordinated from CAP's headquarters at Lancaster were enhanced by additional satellite offices in Hagerhill and Louisa, Kentucky. With the increase, it was obvious that Father Beiting's aim to strengthen and support Appalachian families had come closer to fruition. More people than ever before were provided with services relating to community development, child development, crisis intervention and education.[22]

When Father Beiting started the community development program years ago, he taught poor people how to farm a plot of land and produce food to feed their families. He envisioned that someday many Appalachians would be able to use this approach as one of their elements of survival. The value of his foresight came about when the CAP-created Farm Support Program experienced remarkable growth into the early nineties. Companies from all over the country were donating seeds in bulk to CAP. In turn, workers and volunteers weighed and packaged vegetable, fruit and flower seeds in labeled envelopes, and distributed them to many thousands of poor families, who had small farms and gardens. Tools and supplies such as fertilizer, pesticides, and canning jars and other CAP assistance made it appealing for the poor to help themselves in this fashion. Not only were they able to feed their families, but also a sense

Courtesy Christian Appalachian Project

Monsignor Beiting observes a group of children who are attending a CAP development program.

of community had developed, as the people worked coopera-tively with each other and shared the bounty of their land.

At the time Father Beiting first established programs for children, they were aimed to improve their quality of life. By the early nineties, CAP child development initiatives were rec-ognized at the national level, and included home-based pro-grams for infants, followed by in-center learning experiences relating to pre-school children. Further evidence of the effec-tiveness of these programs was the research of public school teachers, which confirmed that children from the Christian Ap-palachian Project centers were well-prepared for kindergarten and first grade.

Beiting's strong commitment to CAP's crisis intervention program was further evidenced by the increase of outreach offices that were helping more people through difficult times.

While crisis intervention services met immediate physical and emotional needs, they also guided people to long-term solutions of their problems. For example, outreach caseworkers helped folks take an important step in dealing with their financial problems. They provided various approaches to budgeting, which enabled the poor to learn how to stretch their meager resources to the limit.

One of the most fruitful decisions Father Beiting made when he first came to Appalachia was the development of educational programs for the region's youth. During the early nineties, CAP provided a greater diversity of offerings for these young people. A notable addition at this time was the introduction of a program that emphasized awareness of the environment. Camps Andrew Jackson and Shawnee offered environmental education as part of a cooperative venture with local public schools. Through a variety of hands-on activities, young people learned about their environment and the interaction of all species.

In the beginning of 1994, Father Beiting took another approach toward creating more job opportunities for the Appalachian people. After a series of meetings with his administrative staff, outside consultants, and area business people, he established the Mountain Economic Development Fund, Inc. Beiting and CAP's board of directors determined that this community development financing entity would promote, through funding and technical assistance, the formation and expansion of businesses, and subsequent employment opportunities.[23]

The Mountain Economic Development Fund demonstrated its value right from the start. In the first 30 days of operation, it made $35,000 in business investments that led to over twenty jobs. In less than one year, the fund and its community-based Board of Directors received applications for projects that totaled more than $3,000,000 to employ over 1,000 people, highlighting the need for capital investment in the Appalachian region.

Right from the beginning, MEDF took creative steps to serve as many people as possible. First, Grant Satterly, who had previous experience as a financial manager in government and private ventures, was hired as executive director. Satterly recently said, "I felt privileged to work for the Mountain Economic Development Fund where our successes could be measured not only in financial, but human terms. Father Beiting once said to me that the best welfare was a good, steady job, and MEDF was proud to be an instrument attempting to deliver that welfare."[24]

An important aspect of this operation was the deep and personal interest in the ongoing success of each of its clients. It provided a variety of educational and technical resources, such as consultant services and a steady flow of information on personnel management, bookkeeping, financial reports, etc. For clients that needed more specialized help, MEDF referred them to small business assistance centers at the University of Kentucky, Eastern Kentucky University, and Morehead State University. In addition, MEDF employed a full time marketing professional who provided personal assistance to businesses it had funded.

Father Beiting was enthusiastic about MEDF's accomplishments. Loans assisted a variety of industries that included indoor-outdoor furniture factories, a forage seed product company, a sport boat manufacturer, as well as producers of wood moldings, flooring, and other specialty products. Other loans contributed to the expansion of a data entry service company and a plastics factory that moved a segment of its operation from Florida to eastern Kentucky.

Even though these initiatives were evident as business opportunities and jobs increased, Beiting believed that much more had to be done. He called out to responsible citizens of financial means to get involved, and informed them that a new concept of economic development was needed in Eastern Kentucky. Since the return on investment would not be as great in Appalachia as in other places of the country, he felt that concerned citizens who wanted to help the region should not put profits before Christian deeds.

Ever since Father Beiting founded CAP, part of its mission was to assist other charitable groups involved in education, emergency assistance, health care and housing through human development grants. During the nineties, other charitable organizations that had helped the needy beyond CAP's service area were on the increase. However, many of these groups needed assistance themselves to carry out their work for the poor. This led CAP to expand its Human Development Grants program. "By providing these nonprofit groups with grants, CAP was able to more effectively assist people throughout Eastern Kentucky, parts of Tennessee and West Virginia," program manager Sheila Helton said.[25]

For the Christian Appalachian Project, it was important that each local organization commit itself to its area for an extended period. As a result, CAP developed long-standing relationships with many of these groups who were doing outstanding service. In addition, CAP provided matching grants to encourage them to become involved in alternate fund raising methods. The flexibility and diversity of the Human Development Grants Program also gave impetus for these local charities to refine and restate their mission and prioritize for the future, which enabled CAP to expand its services to other groups.

One such organization that Father Beiting often referred to was Interfaith of Bell County, Inc., that came about as a result of a 1977 flood in the Pineville, Kentucky area. At that time, Beiting, his workers and CAP volunteers were among the many people who helped the flood victims. Subsequently, leaders of the local churches organized Interfaith to deal with the aftermath of this catastrophe. Once these needs were met, it was felt that the organization was too important to disband, and Interfaith of Bell County incorporated in 1978. Since then, it has continued to respond to the needs of another disaster—poverty.[26]

As an example of Interfaith's effectiveness, in 1994, it used CAP's funding to support a food pantry, utility and rent assistance, and eyeglass service for over 2,500 people. Impressed with what Interfaith had accomplished, Beiting said, "I see this action as a strong Christian foundation for every community in Appalachia, to help more needy people regain a sense of dignity and self worth." Consequently, funding local cooperative Christian groups and nonprofit organizations by the Human Development Grants program became an important function of CAP's mission.

As with all Christian Appalachian Project programs in the nineties, the work of Operation Sharing rose to the challenge of a changing and expanding service area. By 1994, Operation Sharing had reached all of the thirteen Appalachian mountain range states. At this time, CAP received approximately $17 million worth of donated goods and materials from corporations, industry and individuals for Operation Sharing to distribute. By 1995, CAP's contribution to these Appalachian states and beyond increased to $20 million, with Beiting calling for a projection of $50 million by the year 2000.

In late 1995, Mike McLaughlin told Father Beiting that while he wanted to continue working with CAP, he was ready for a change in his professional direction. He asked to step down as president, and give his full attention to Operation Sharing. Beiting and McLaughlin, over the course of several meetings, agreed that Mike would serve as director of this program. The future needs and addition of warehouses in satellite centers and added personnel were a challenge that appealed to McLaughlin, who felt that he could attain the projected increase that Beiting had established.[27]

By early spring of 1996, CAP's Board of Directors appointed Mike Sanders as president. Sanders, a very capable administrator, did an outstanding job as senior director of programs in Floyd County. Upon accepting the position as president, Sanders expressed his gratitude for the opportunity to continue carrying on the work of Father Beiting.

Also, in 1996, Operation Sharing distributed in-kind donations to over 1,200 churches, schools, and other organizations. As soon as CAP was alerted that donations were on their way, plans were made for immediate pick up. "In one day and out the next" was Operation Sharing's motto. There were many requests, yet none was too difficult for CAP to satisfy. For example, a struggling town in West Virginia received instant attention when Operation Sharing sent truckloads of roofing materials, insulation, paint, clothing, food, and a multitude of other useful supplies. Championed by Father Beiting, this initiative was one of CAP's many contributions to the needy, which brought the people of the community together in a way they never experienced before.[28]

On another occasion, one of CAP's largest contributors donated 240,000 books (children's books, classics, cookbooks and fiction) for Operation Sharing to distribute to literacy programs, school districts, and other groups throughout the thirteen Appalachian states. In addition, books were sent to Indian reservations out west. Kentucky's Family Resource Centers also became recipients of Operation Sharing contributions. Established as part of the Kentucky Educational Reform Act of 1990, these centers were located in communities where at least twenty percent of the children qualified for free or reduced lunches. By being partners with Family Resource Centers, CAP felt confident that materials were given to the truly needy.

In addition, many of CAP's own programs were enhanced by in-kind donations to Operation Sharing. For instance, one company sent seventeen tractor-trailer loads of building insulation for use in CAP's home repair programs, which included WorkFest. Operation Sharing also fulfilled its primary mission by acting as a partner with non-profit organizations (churches, schools, etc.) in distributing materials and supplies to their communities. By the end of 1996, Operation Sharing had

Courtesy Christian Appalachian Project

Rev. Beiting and Mike Sanders observe a CAP home repair crew at work.

grown beyond everyone's expectation, and Beiting was excited about the direction of this program, which served approximately 800,000 people that year in the thirteen Appalachian mountain range states.[29]

During this time, Father Beiting continued to play an important role for bringing economic opportunities to Appalachia. On one occasion, he heard about the "ecology home," which was manufactured by a Florida company and shipped to other countries to replace those destroyed by natural disasters. Made partially from recycled plastic, and considered environmentally sound, one of these homes was purchased by Beiting for a new camp that CAP had developed on Yatesville Lake near Louisa. Impressed with its unique features of low cost and inexpensive upkeep, the Appalachian Development Corporation, CAP's for-profit subsidiary, purchased fifteen homes in 1996 to be built on property next to the Appalachian Village in Berea. At that time, a three-bedroom home cost approximately $300 per month, based on a twelve-year mortgage. Another feature of this "ecology housing" venture was that it also created employment. Beiting and ADC made a commitment to construct sixty more homes in Appalachia. Bill Kane, founder of Eagle Plastics, the company that manufactured the home, supported Beiting's economic growth efforts, by opening a small factory in Prestonsburg, providing more jobs for local people.[30]

In December of 1996, Father Beiting received the Kentucky Governor's Economic Development Leadership Award. At the banquet, Governor Paul Patton stated: "This recognition is given to those individuals whose vision and leadership have been instrumental in improving Kentucky's local, regional, and statewide economy."[31]

For the Beiting clan, the Awards Banquet was remembered as a family affair. In attendance were his brothers, sisters, and their spouses, for he wanted them to share in this achievement. Father Beiting never forgot the selfless support of his family, who always came to his assistance in time of need, even though they did not live in Appalachia and had to travel long distances. As he remembers, "It was this closeness that got me through some rough times."[32]

He especially acknowledged his sister, Sister Mary Martha

Courtesy Father Beiting Collection

In December 1996, Monsignor Beiting accepts an award from Governor Paul Patton for his vision and leadership in improving Kentucky's local, regional, and statewide economy.

Beiting, SND, who over the years faithfully supported his work. She cared for needy children at St. Aloysius orphanage in Cincinnati, Ohio, and at times, he turned to her for help to look after orphans from Appalachia. Sister Mary Martha also taught in his summer Bible school program, and collected as well as distributed goods for the poor.[33]

During the first week of January 1997, Father Beiting traveled to Florida to discuss the progress of an economic development project. He then met with religious leaders, lectured at a seminar, and came back home by the end of the week to continue work on the planning of a facility for adults with disabilities. In the weeks that followed, Beiting's initiatives and actions recurred in steady and rapid succession. Appalachia's society was still struggling with many problems, and more people came to him for help each new day. He provided for the homeless by giving them shelter, job training, counseling and other assistance. There were others who sought help, such as single mothers, and he offered them childcare services and opportunities to gain employment, or attend school in order to stay off welfare. The unfortunate and continuing saga of alcoholism, suicide and abuse led youth and adults to seek help from Beiting. He would also go to places he had never heard of before—backcountry hollows where the poor could only dream of a better life, and opportunities were never available.

In the early part of March 1997, major areas of southern Ohio and northern Kentucky encountered extensive flooding. Families were uprooted as the Ohio River, along with tributaries and low-lying creeks, overflowed. In his usual uplifting manner, Beiting rallied his organization and distributed cleaning supplies, food, clothing, furniture, etc. to the many thousands of people who were devastated by the flood.[34]

As other people his age retired, Father Beiting continued a full schedule as pastor of three mission churches, (St. Jude, Louisa; St. John Neuman, Hode; St. Stephen, Inez) and remained as Chairman of CAP's Board of Directors. He had more enthusiasm for his job than when he was 26. He persevered to make every day complete, fitting in more activities than any ordinary person would, and his resilient spirit continued to inspire employees and volunteers. Among these admirers was Richard Ginn, who had an excellent grasp of Beiting's never ending involvement with CAP activities. Ginn, assistant director of the CAP operations in Louisa, who served as a minister in Ohio before moving back to his home state of Kentucky, said: "He's the greatest humanitarian I have ever met. I was hired to help relieve some of his workload and found out that you don't relieve him. He'll take the opportunity to change gears and pick up more work!"[35] Beiting not only impressed Ginn with the way he handled the hectic daily challenges, but other staff members as well. Rose Price, director of the Hagerhill office said, "He is unique by being in tune with the change of time. His knowledge and accuracy of keeping a pulse on the total CAP organization is incredible."[36]

At the end of May 1997, Ottawa University, Kansas, honored Father Beiting with the Meeker Award. This was granted annually to individuals whose dedication to Christianity and education mirrors the characteristics of Baptist missionaries Jothan and Eleanor Meeker. They are famous for their work with the Ottawa tribe of Native Americans, which led them to found Ottawa, Kansas, the First Baptist Church, and the university.

Jerod Huguenot, an Ottawa University graduate who served as a CAP volunteer counselor, had nominated Beiting for the award. "Jerod was really moved by the work Father Beiting had done to start the organization and the faith it has taken to sustain it," said Kathy Kluesener, director of CAP's volunteer program. Kluesener, who accompanied Beiting to Ottawa, Kansas, for the award ceremonies, said, "You see a real spirit of ecumenism coming through when a Baptist institution honors a Catholic priest."[37]

Interspersed throughout Beiting's involvement with spiritual and humanitarian events and activities has always been his passion for writing. His eleventh book, *A Time of Crisis...A Time for Christ* was published in the latter part of 1997.[38] As with his earlier books, Beiting wrote about the people who were dear to his heart, the oppressed, the voiceless, and the marginalized.

In 1998, he continued to spiritually nourish the people of Appalachia, and strived more than ever to mobilize the needy to help themselves. Each day he spent countless hours undertaking the many responsibilities that confronted him. Besides his daily offering of mass, and other spiritual activities, he gave endlessly to make sure that the poor—adults, children, the disabled, and elderly—were provided with a semblance of decency in their lives.

Because of his multifaceted contributions, recognition of Beiting's work continued to come his way. In December of 1998, he was a recipient of the Lincoln Award, given by Northern Kentucky University for his "commitment to service, fidelity to noble causes and a sense of turning challenges into opportunities." This was one of many recognitions during the nineties for his contributions, which included honorary doctorate degrees from: Xavier University, Cincinnati, Ohio; Spalding University, Louisville, Kentucky; St. Joseph College, Cincinnati, Ohio; and Walham's Hall, Ogdensburg, New York.[39]

Today, after fifty years of spiritual and humanitarian work, the inspiration that Father Beiting has generated through his dedication to the people is unlimited. Yet, he knows there is much more that needs to be done. Poverty, which escalated for too many years, has become a more complex problem that appears to be bottomless, as areas of Appalachia continue to be the "poorest of the poor" in our nation. This pains him, for he is concerned with the mounting societal changes that are presenting greater obstacles for the indigent, namely the children. In some places where CAP is servicing two out of three children who live in poverty, many lack motivation and begin at an early age to develop a defeatist attitude, which makes it difficult to improve their lives. "Too many of these children are not provided with worthwhile opportunities or choices for growing up," Beiting says, "they come from families who are unable, for one reason or another, to help themselves escape poverty." Without effective guidance, the children are left with a feeling of abandonment toward any hope for their future.

On one occasion, Father Beiting remembers a heartbreaking glimpse of hopelessness when he met a young boy who was sitting in a rocking chair on the porch of a small backwoods general store. Wanting to gain an understanding about the boy's aspirations in life, Beiting asked him what he wanted to be when he grew up. The boy answered, "Well, I reckon I'm gonna rock in a rockin' chair like my pappy does."

Historically, the lack of effective parental role models has also been a deterrent for Appalachian children to survive the harsh realities of their impoverishment. Beiting says, "Some children grow up too fast not realizing the consequences of their actions. They don't know of any other way to live a better life." Unable to cope with everyday frustrations, self-destruction starts at an early age, and in certain cases the depravity of their situation leads to teen suicide. Father Beiting remembers when he came across a boy, who at age five drank alcohol, smoked cigarettes, and swore like a trooper." He and his four siblings lived with their mother in a broken-down trailer. Beiting and CAP came to the rescue. Even though many obstacles had to be overcome, guided commitment, caring and concern over a long term by this priest, his staff and volunteers made a positive impact on the boy and his family.

There is yet another concern that Father Beiting has for children and sees on the increase abuse inflicted by others. On one occasion, a mother, her four-year old daughter and three-year old son, came to his door seeking help after her husband was put in jail for sexually abusing the older child. Since the mother and her children did not have a place to stay, Beiting took them to a CAP Abuse Center, where shelter along with physical and emotional support services were provided. In time, the professional staff and personnel were able to make it possible for this family to ease their burden.

In trying to improve the lives of children who have come from backgrounds afflicted with many disadvantages, Beiting has set a precedent by providing a diversity of educational, social, health and dental care programs. Included in each program are prevention, intervention and treatment services for thousands of children annually. Without this comprehensive approach of support, the magnitude of poverty would be much greater in those areas that the Christian Appalachian Project serves.

Father Beiting not only continues to be concerned with the conditions of poverty that affect the young, but also the rest of Appalachia's society. Still operating on the philosophy of "helping people to help themselves," CAP gives emphasis to human development, addressing both short and long-term needs. Education, health care, and other social or family strengthening services are functioning at their optimal level, as more young people and adults are benefiting from CAP's variety of offerings. Attention is given to teen pregnancy, sex issues, substance abuse, family dysfunction and other matters that relate to young people and adults. Counseling services are available for individuals and families. Tutoring of teenagers and adults working toward high school equivalency certification or literacy instruction are in constant demand. Life skills training and supported employment opportunities for persons with disabilities, have given many a foothold on a decent way of life. Interwoven throughout the CAP programs is a full complement of services for the elderly. Also, CAP's emergency services continue to provide temporary assistance (short-term) to help the needy get back on their feet and become self-supporting.

One of Father Beiting's top priorities is to keep students in school, since Eastern Kentucky has one of the highest dropout rates in the nation. Consequently, CAP has utilized its Youth

Centers to provide a wide range of services that help teenagers become responsible citizens and work for effective self-change, in spite of their living in poverty. Beiting also offers college scholarships for high school students who financially cannot afford it. Through the years many of these students graduated from college and became respectable leaders and effective citizens.

Father Beiting has not stopped there, and when another need appears, the Christian Appalachian Project initiates a new program or service. Working with all levels of poverty, CAP continues to examine the causes, and develops the processes that bring about solutions to people's problems. In turn, Beiting and his organization have built a strong foundation for change, so that the needy of Appalachia can achieve a better life. CAP has done this by providing a most comprehensive offering of programs and services that focus on the essentials of life: food, clothing, education, health and health care, housing and employment.

As a result of Beiting's dynamic leadership, the Christian Appalachian Project has become one of the largest non-profit organizations in America, offering a greater diversity of programs and services affecting over one million people a year. Throughout his years in Appalachia, up to fifty thousand volunteers have joined Beiting and his workers to fight poverty and inspire hope. Almost fifteen hundred other non-profit organizations and groups are annually assisted by CAP to provide direct services to the needy in their own local communities. Also, contributions by CAP to these groups have nearly reached fifty million dollars a year. Not to be overlooked are the countless numbers of donors from throughout the United States, who have faithfully contributed, whether financially or in-kind, so that this organization could effectively carry out its mission.[40]

Despite Father Beiting's accomplishments, he feels that his

work is far from finished. The widespread human suffering that has dominated this part of America continues to be daunting, for too many Appalachians are still living in poverty. Yet, this priest's resolve grows stronger each day, and he prays that "God will give me the strength to continue working for His people in Appalachia until my last breath."[41]

Father Beiting

Courtesy W. Brunner–Berea, Kentucky

A VISION FOR THE FUTURE

As the new millennium has been introduced, one cannot help think of the immeasurable impact Father Ralph William Beiting has made on many of Appalachia's people, and others as well. This extraordinary priest has set a course for his inter-denominational organization that ensures a strong future as it continues to face the challenges of poverty. Yet, he dreams of how much more can be accomplished if more Americans come forward with renewed vigor to help the growing number of poor people. One way he sees this happening "is through spiritual faith, by joining Christ's work as volunteers." He wants people to know that "No matter how insignificant their role in life may appear to them, if they enthusiastically surrender to God, marvelous things can happen."[1]

Reflecting on his own life, Beiting knows how much God has influenced humanity. He cites that even his own skills and the organizational acumen of the people who joined him to achieve many endeavors, came about through the grace of God. This includes the momentous contributions that his volunteers of the past and present have produced, and leads him to call upon the young and old of today to join his crusade.

Whether a young person is finishing school or becomes involved in a vocation, volunteerism provides intangibles that are both rewarding and self-fulfilling. There are also opportunities for adults to volunteer later on in life, after their children have grown up. "These people have a chance to step away from the great materialistic rush and make a difference in another direction," Beiting says. "It is admirable when people offer their skills and experiences to help ensure that the underprivileged receive assistance." He strongly feels volunteers are a vision of hope for the needy guiding them to rise above their unfortunate circumstances.

With ecumenism being an important part of Father Beiting's work, he continues to set his sights on religious cooperation. He aspires for a community of solidarity, where all Christian organizations strive toward a common goal of following Jesus. Undeniably, Beiting loves his faith and treasures it, but he knows that "God wants people to love and respect one another and not be strangers, much less enemies to those of other persuasions." He further recognizes that people who are not of his faith also love God sincerely, and do good work to conform their lives fully to the Lord. That is why he is calling for the combining of efforts in which persons from all religions need to take action, and not be observers. "They should extend their hands and touch people of other faiths, walk the path together, and fight the common foe side by side."

When Father Beiting talks about his vision for the future, he feels that a most compelling challenge is commitment. He points out that total commitment has made a difference in his life without limiting his work. To many people, this may appear to be a difficult task, and Beiting expresses concern that it is common to find the easy way out of whatever challenge they face. "Our society finds it more palatable to change religions, marriage partners, and almost anything that is not pleasant or agreeable. This is why total commitment of faith is imperative, otherwise, the ills of poverty will be too difficult to solve." He further reminds us that "To do God's work here on Earth, one must be able to persevere, which is essential in order to help improve the lives of others."

Beiting's own journey through Appalachia has been one of perseverance and spiritual gratification that goes beyond words and measurement. Despite the many discouraging conditions that are synonymous with poverty, his devotion will never cease. "This is where I shall work, even though the parishes are small, the distances great, and the resources limited, as long as it is the work of God," he says.

Ever since he arrived in Appalachia, Father Beiting's love for the region has never waned. He recently said, "To love Appalachia, one has to have a sense of loyalty." Whatever the difficulties, he feels that the people themselves must aim to eliminate the many barriers, which means unquestionable loyalty to the mountain country. He says this with great compassion, because his own dedication and love are indisputably evident.

Father Beiting's hope is that more participants from the region commit themselves and make Appalachia a better place to live. His goal is to stimulate Appalachians to change their attitudes, "because the indifference of people is disappointing." He sees a lot of wealth, yet the unwillingness to share and make it productive saddens him. This type of attitude deters growth of the region, and if it continues, Appalachia will move toward a future of greater uncertainty. It also hurts him to see poor people willing to follow a journey of everlasting handouts, and remain in the doldrums of a directionless life. He feels that they need to develop strength in their character in order to make changes for the better, or the cycle of deteriorating circumstances will continue to affect every fiber of their existence.

Finally, with environment as a dominant theme of his work for the future, he says, "It is easy to get discouraged at times.

The filth and debris that still scatters Appalachia's roads and countryside are an atrocious affront to the beauty God put there. Sometimes you see all these things and wish to goodness they would be different. There could be beauty, excitement, and love. Yet, I think that it shall only come if we, who care and love Appalachia, will be more responsible for its future."

Regardless of his anguish, Beiting's undying commitment is obvious when he says, "Appalachia is still a beautiful place, and does not pretend it is greater than it is." He continues to love this mountain country, and has no intention of walking away. Instead, he will persist to nurse it to greater strength, and help the people toward positive change. Beiting is not living in a make-believe world, but one where sin and ugliness are present, as well as beauty and goodness. "That is what the Lord asks of us: to love the truth, and seek the beauty," he states. "If we do that and are loyal and faithful, it will make a difference."

Through almost five decades of serving in Appalachia, Father Beiting's missionary example has inspired a nationwide network of faithful donors. These are people who have contributed through financial and in-kind gifts, as their support has played an important role in his evangelization throughout Appalachia. Yet, as we look to the future, more requests are made of donors who support charitable organizations, such as the Christian Appalachian Project. The reasons for the increase are many: government has cut back on its efforts of helping the less fortunate, corporations are limiting their gifts, and even foundations have experienced a strain in giving. Topping this off, today's society has a tendency to overlook charity, and at times, views it with suspicion.

However, Father Beiting hopes CAP supporters understand

that each contribution makes a difference. He is sincere when he says, "It doesn't matter whether a person gives only a few dollars or much more. The importance is that it comes from their heart. Generosity is two-fold. First, there are the material things they contribute. Beyond that, there is the love that makes them give, and God uses this in a marvelous way to bring about change." In turn, the goodness in these givers has been an inspiration for Father Beiting to carry on his ministry. To him, charity and generosity are wonderful aspects of human life, and a beautiful continuation of love for God. It makes people think of others more than themselves, and at the same time is very rewarding.

In setting his sights on the future, Beiting looks at the past and talks about the foundation established through his leadership and spiritual guidance. He realizes that what started will not stop, "Because there are too many people who truly care and love God to keep the spirit alive." In essence, he is paying homage to all who have helped. "This is why recognition should not be a monument to one, but a wonderful applause to the work of many, who have come together in carrying out the good deeds Christ has called for."

Father Beiting is realistic about the impact he and his workers have had on Appalachia. "We are not the whole answer to overcoming poverty, just part of it. Other people will stand on our shoulders to reach higher, but they would not have got there without us establishing a foundation." He further emphasizes that the helpers of tomorrow must also love and give unselfishly, so that those who come after them will be able to build upon their work. Beiting views the results as their gift of power from Christ. "We are not the heroes, only the laborers and servants. If we have done well, then marvelous things will take place because of God, who formed and fashioned us."

This dedicated priest calls out for people to join Christ and observe His life of love and sacrifice. In turn, they should accept the invitation to walk with Him alongside the multitude of followers, and show to the world a sight of devotion, loyalty, determination, commitment, and courage that will eventually change the attitude of others. In viewing Beiting's goal for the coming years, he urges the people to live as Christ lived. "We're not going to make this a better place through money, power, or material things, but by faith, love, and God. Then people will achieve what they could have never done by themselves."

When we look at Father Beiting's gift to society, we see an integration of spiritual and humanitarian contributions. This man of God has had a tremendous influence in bringing out the highest of religious and social standards of those persons he has touched. In an age when many raise questions about the role of priests, it is interesting to note that from the beginning of his ministry, he fully committed himself to all people.

Father Beiting sees priesthood as the greatest gift ever given to him, and praises God for making this possible and fruitful. Through all the years, his fidelity has endured, and his loyalty remains constant. He proclaims that priesthood is one of the most exciting and rewarding vocations on earth. It has given him the opportunity to devote his life to Jesus. He demonstrates his responsibility to the human family in such a way that he sees Christ in every one of them. Finally, Beiting likens priesthood to a dramatic exposition of how much good can come when one is faithful to his calling.

Since the future presents unpredictable challenges, Father Beiting knows that his faith and courage must sustain him just like the Apostles, when they were told by Jesus, "Come, follow me." They had the courage to do so, and the whole world has never been the same. In a similar way, Ralph William Beiting came to Appalachia to spread Christ's message of faith, hope, and love. It has been a journey of great achievement and fulfillment. His dear friend and colleague, Father Lou Brinker, calls Father Beiting "the embodiment of what a priest should be like, who has that rare wisdom to exhilarate people of all faiths, with a vision for the future."[2]

Courtesy W. Brunner—Berea, Kentucky

Father Beiting preaching in one of the communities on the Ohio River.

NOTES
AND
REFERENCES

Notes and References

CHAPTER 1

1. *Called to the Mountains*, the autobiography of Reverend Ralph W. Beiting and the Christian Appalachian Project, Lancaster, Kentucky: CAP, 1993, p.7.

2. Interview with author, April 12, 1996.

3. Interview with author, April 12, 1996.

4. Interview with author, April 13, 1996.

5. *Called to the Mountains*, 1993, p.9.

6. Ibid.

7. Interview with author, April 13, 1996.

8. *Dreams of Faith, Reverend Beiting's Dream for Appalachia* by Reverend Ralph W. Beiting with Tom Pelletier, Lancaster, Kentucky: Christian Appalachian Project, 1992, p.66.

9. *Appalachia . . . A Special Place . . . A Bridge of Hope*, by Reverend Ralph W. Beiting, Lancaster, Kentucky Christian Appalachian Project, 1990, p. 53-54.

10. *Called to the Mountains*, Lancaster, Kentucky: Christian Appalachian Project, 1993, p.16.

11. Interview with author, April 12, 1996.

12. *Called to the Mountains*, Lancaster, Kentucky: CAP, 1993, p.21.

13. Interview with author, April 13, 1996.

14. Interview with author, April 13, 1996.

15. *Called to the Mountains*, Lancaster, Kentucky: CAP, 1993. p.19.

16. Letter from Ralph William Beiting to Sister Jullita, November 7, 1946.

17. Interview with author, April 14, 1996.

18. Interview with author, April 14, 1996.

19. Interview with author, April 12, 1996.

20. Interview with author, April 13, 1996.

21. Father Beiting's sisters' interview with author, April 18, 1996.

22. Mary Lou Deavy interview with author, April 18, 1996.

23. Interview with author, April 14, 1996.

24 Interview with author, March, 1996.

25 Interview with author, March, 1996.

26 Interview with author, March, 1996.

27. Interview with author, April 14, 1996.

28. Interview with author, April 12, 1996.

29. Interview with author, May, 1996.

30. Interview with author, May, 1996.

31. Interview with author, May, 1996.

32. Interview with author, May, 1996.

33. Interview with author, May, 1996.

CHAPTER 2

1. Covington Diocesan seminarians generally received their training in the Catholic Educational College Network of the Archdiocese of Cincinnati.

2. Interview with author, May, 1996.

3. Interview with author, May, 1996.

4. Interview with author, May, 1996.

5. Interview with author, May, 1996.

6. Letter from Ralph William Beiting to Sister Jullita, September 28, 1946.

7. Interview with author, May, 1996.

8. Glenmary Home Missioners headquarters are in Cincinnati, Ohio.

9. Father Bob Berson served as President of the Glenmary Home Missioners from 1965 – 1971, and 1975 – 1983.

10. Interview with author, May, 1996.

11. Interview with author, May, 1996.

12. Interview with author, May, 1996.

13. Interview with author, May, 1996.

14. Interview with author, May, 1996.

15. *Unpublished Autobiography of Ministry in Eastern Kentucky* by Father Beiting, who wrote recollections of his priesthood at the request of Sister Mary Kevan Seibert, SND, Chancellor and Archivist of the Catholic Diocese of Lexington, February 8, 1993.

16. Ibid.

17. Covington Diocesan Archives.

18. Interview with author, May, 1996.

19. *Unpublished Autobiography of Ministry in Eastern Kentucky*, by Father Ralph W. Beiting, Feburary 8, 1993.

20. St. Michael's School endured through the years, and in 1995, the school, now known as Our Lady of the Mountains, celebrated its fiftieth anniversary.

21. Previously, the Covington diocese had bought land with an old mansion, built at the turn of the century by a pioneer coal baron named John C. Mayo.

22. Sisters of Divine Providence ran St. Michaels School and the hospital.

23. Loretta Lynn: *Coal Miner's Daughter*, by Loretta Lynn and George Vecsey, Chicago: Regenery, 1996.

24. Interview with author, April 12, 1996.

25. Interview with author, April 13, 1996.

26. Interview with author, March, 1996.

27. Interview with author, March, 1996.

28. Interview with author, April 12, 1996.

29. Letter from Ralph William Beiting to Sister Jullita, October 7, 1947.

30. Letter from Ralph William Beiting to Sister Jullita, November 2, 1947. These letters along with others contained Beiting's impressions of his professors,

studies and work at Catholic University and the Washington, D.C. area.
31. Interview with author, April 14, 1996.
32. St. Matthew Cathedral is the seat of Washington's Archbishop.
33. Interview with author, June, 1996.
34. Interview with author, June, 1996.
35. Interview with author, June, 1996.
36. Interview with author, June, 1996.
37. Interview with author, June, 1996.
38. Interview with author, June, 1996.
39. Interview with author, June, 1996.
40. Interview with author, June, 1996.
41. Interview with author, June, 1996.
42. Interview with author, June, 1996.
43. Interview with author, June, 1996.
44. Interview with author, June, 1996.

CHAPTER 3
1. Interview with author, April 12, 1996.
2. Dorothy Noll interview with author, April 18, 1996.
3. Interview with author, April 12, 1996.
4. Interview with author, May, 1996.
5. Beiting brothers and sisters interview with author, April 18, 1996.
6. *Unpublished Autobiography of Ministry in Eastern Kentucky*, by Father Beiting, February 8, 1993.
7. Interview with author, April 13, 1996.
8. Interview with author, April 13, 1996.
9. Interview with author, April 14, 1996.
10. Interview with author, May, 1996.
11. Interview with author, May, 1996.
12. *Unpublished Autobiography of Ministry in Eastern Kentucky*, by Father Beiting, February 8, 1993.
13. *Unpublished Autobiography of Ministry in Eastern Kentucky*, by Father Beiting, February 8, 1993.
14. Clare Booth Luce later became Ambassador to Italy from 1953 to 1957. She was the first American woman to represent the United States to a foreign country.
15. Interview with author, May, 1996.
16. Interview with author, May, 1996.
17. *Unpublished Autobiography of Ministry in Eastern Kentucky*, by Father Beiting, February 8, 1993.

CHAPTER 4
1. *Pilgrimage of a Country Preacher . . . A Journey to the Holy Land of Appalachia*, by Father Ralph W. Beiting with Tom Pelletier, Lancaster, Kentucky: CAP, 1995, p.9.
2. Ibid., p. 10
3. Ibid., p.10

4.   Ibid., p. 9

5.   Don Beiting interview with author, April 18, 1996.

6.   Interview with author, June, 1996

7.   Interview with author, June, 1996

8.   Interview with author, June, 1996

9.   *Unpublished Autobiography of Ministry in Eastern Kentucky*, by Father Beiting, February 8, 1993.

10.   *Pilgrimage of a Country Preacher . . . A Journey to the Holy Land of Appalachia*, by Father Ralph W. Beiting with Tom Pelletier, Lancaster, Kentucky: CAP, 1995, p. 17.

11.   Ibid., p. 18

12.   *Promises to Keep, A Vision for Appalachia*, by Father Ralph W. Beiting with Tom Pelletier, Lancaster, Kentucky: 1991, p. 18-19.

13.   Interview with author, June, 1996.

14.   Interview with author, June, 1996.

15.   Interview with author, June, 1996.

16.   Interview with author, June, 1996.

17.   Interview with author, June, 1996.

18.   Meetings were held at the homes of Adolph Feldman, Annie Smith and Connie Miller.

19.   Interview with author, June, 1996.

20.   Judge Calico later sold his house for volunteers to use as a dormitory.

21.   Interview with author, June, 1996.

22.   Interview with author, June, 1996.

23.   *Unpublished Autobiography of Ministry in Eastern Kentucky*, by Father Beiting, February 8, 1993.

24.   Interview with author, June, 1996.

25.   Interview with author, June, 1996.

26.   *Pilgrimage of a Country Preacher . . . A Journey to the Holy Land of Appalachia*, by Father Ralph W. Beiting with Tom Pelleteir, Lancaster, Kentucky: 1995, p.44.

27.   Interview with author, June, 1996.

28.   Interview with author, June, 1996.

29.   Interview with author, June, 1996.

30.   Interview with author, June, 1996.

31.   Interview with author, June, 1996.

32.   Father Kamlage interview with author, April 17, 1996.

33.   Father Kamlage interview with author, April 17, 1996.

34.   Father Rolf interview with author, April 16, 1996.

35.   Interview with author, April 13, 1996.

36.   Father Rolf interview with author, April 16, 1996.

37.   Christian Appalachian Project, 1990, pgs. 15 – 16.

38.   Interview with author, May, 1996.

39.   Interview with author, May, 1996.

40.   Interview with author, April 12, 1996.

41.   Mary Ann Bullock interview with author, April 9, 1996.

42.   Interview with author, April 14, 1996.

43.   *Night Comes to the Cumberlands*, by Harry M. Caudill., Boston: Little &

Brown, 1962, p. 172.

44. Interview with author, April 14, 1996.

45. *Promises to Keep*, by Father Ralph W. Beiting with Tom Pelletier, Lancaster, Kentucky: CAP, 1991, pp. 18-19.

46. Interview with author, May, 1996.

47. Interview with author, May, 1996.

48. Father Kamlage interview with author, April 17, 1996.

49. Interview with author, May, 1996.

50. Interview with author, May, 1996.

51. Berea College, Kentucky was founded in 1855.

52. Interview with author, May, 1996.

53. Father Kamlage interview with author, April 17, 1996.

54. *Unpublished Autobiography of Ministry in Eastern Kentucky*, by Father Ralph W. Beiting, February 8, 1993.

55. Interview with author, June, 1996.

56. Interview with author, June, 1996.

57. Interview with author, June, 1996.

58. Interview with author, June, 1996.

59. Interview with author, June, 1996.

60. Interview with author, June, 1996.

61. Interview with author, June, 1996.

62. Interview with author, June, 1996.

63. Interview with author, June, 1996.

64. *Unpublished Autobiography of Ministry in Eastern Kentucky*, by Father Ralph W. Beiting, February 8, 1993.

65. *The Sign*, National Catholic Magazine, published by the Passionists, Union City, New Jersey: August, 1969, p. 35.

CHAPTER 5

1. Interview with author, June, 1996

2. Interview with author, June, 1996

3. *Unpublished Autobiography of Ministry in Eastern Kentucky*, by Father Ralph Beiting, February 8, 1993.

4. *Unpublished Autobiography of Ministry in Eastern Kentucky*, by Father Ralph Beiting, February 8, 1993.

5. Covington Diocesan Archives information.

6. Interview with author, June, 1996.

7. Interview with author, June, 1996

8. Interview with author, June, 1996

9. Interview with author, June, 1996

10. Interview with author, June, 1996

11. Interview with author, June, 1996

12. Father Hoppenjans interview with author, April 11, 1996.

13. Interview with author, April 13, 1996.

14. Interview with author, April 13, 1996

15. George Purcell interview with author, April 10, 1996.

16. Interview with author, April 13, 1996.

17. Interview with author, April 14, 1996.

18. Dale Anastasi interview with author, April 15, 1996.

19. Interview with author, April 14, 1996.

20. Peggy Gabriel interview with author, April 15, 1996.

21. *Trends in Relative Income: 1964. 1989*, U.S. Department of Commerce, Bureau of Census, Washington, D.C., December, 1991.

22. Peggy Gabriel interview with author, April 15, 1996.

23. Interview with author, April 14, 1996.

24. Doris and Bill Anglin interview with author, April 10, 1996.

25. Interview with author, June, 1996

26. Interview with author, June, 1996

27. Interview with author, June, 1996

28. Interview with author, June, 1996

29. Interview with author, June, 1996

30. Father Hoppenjans4 interview with author, April 11, 1996.

31. Ray Grace interview with author, April 16, 1996.

32. Brothers of Father Beiting interview with author, April 16, 1996.

33. Dale and Marie Anastasi interview with author, April 15, 1996.

34. Interview with author, April 14, 1996.

35. Interview with author, April 14, 1996.

36. After receiving a note from Louis Freeh, Father Beiting visited with him in Washington, D.C. reminiscing about "the good old days."

37. The Lane Bryant Award was one of many he received annually.

38. Dale and Marie Anastasi interview with author, April 15, 1996.

39. George and Wanda Purcell interview with author, April 10, 1996.

40. Dale and Marie Anastasi interview with author, April 15, 1996.

41. Records from the Volunteer Service Program, Christian Appalachian Project, April 15, 1996.

42. Interview with author, April 12, 1996

43. *The Sign,* National Catholic Magazine published by the Passionists, Union City, New Jersey: August, 1969. p. 46.

CHAPTER 6

1. Documents of CAP programs and services provided by Moe Mercier, April 16, 1996.

2. Interview with author, June, 1996.

3. Interview with author, June, 1996.

4. Interview with author, June, 1996.

5. Interview with author, June, 1996.

6. Interview with author, June, 1996.

7. Cincinnati Enquirer (Kentucky Edition), May 28, 1974.

8. Interview with author, June, 1996.

9. Kentucky River Soundings, Christian Appalachian Project, Lancaster, Kentucky: March, 1979, 9 – 12.

10. Interview with author, June, 1996.

11. Moe Mercier interview with author, April 16, 1996.

12. Interview with author, June, 1996.

13. Interview with author, June, 1996.

14. Interview with author, June, 1996.

15. Kathleen Ford Leavell interview with author, April 16, 1996.

16. Interview with author, June, 1996.

17. Interview with author, June, 1996.

18. Interview with author, June, 1996.

19. Moe Mercier interview with author, April 17, 1996.

20. Moe Mercier interview with author, April 17, 1996.

21. Kentucky River Soundings, Christian Appalachian Project, Lancaster, Kentucky: March, 1979, pp. 6-7. *Kentucky River Soundings*, Christian Appalachian Project, Lancaster, Kentucky: July - August, 1979, pgs. 7-10, 19-20.

22. Ibid., July – August, 1979, pp. 13-14.

23. Kentucky River Soundings, Christian Appalachian Project, Lancaster, Kentucky: September 1979, pp. 11-12.

24. Information provided by Human Development Programs and Services. (Moe Mercier), April 17, 1996.

25. Interview with author, June, 1996.

26. Interview with author, June, 1996.

27. Moe Mercier, Kathy Levall, Kathleen Kleusner interview with author, April 16, 1996.

28. Interview with author, June, 1996.

29. The Messenger, Covington Diocesan Monthly Magazine, May 12, 1971.

30. Father Hoppenjans interview with author, April 11, 1996.

31. Interview with author, June, 1996.

32. Cincinnati Enquirer, Kentucky Edition, August 18, 1973.

33. Cincinnati Post, September 12, 1973.

34. Interview with author, June, 1996.

35. Interview with author, June, 1996.

36. Interview with author, April 14, 1996.

37. Marilyn Stefanski interview with author, April 13, 1996.

38. Interview with author, June, 1996.

39. Peggy Gabriel interview with author, April 16, 1996.

40. Interview with author, June, 1996.

41. Dale and Marie Anastasi interview with author, April 15, 1996.

42. Father Louis Brinker interview with author, April 19, 1996.

43. Don Beiting interview with author, April 18, 1996.

44. Father John Rolf interview with author, April 16,1996.

45. Interview with author, June, 1996.

46. The Kentucky Post, July 1, 1979.

47. Interview with author.

48. Soldier of the Revolution, 1977, and *Adventures of Daniel Boone*, 1977, Christian Appalachian Project, Lancaster, Kentucky.

49. Interview with author, June, 1996.

50. Interview with author, June, 1996.

CHAPTER 7

1. Interview with author, June, 1996.

2. Berea College Records, May 1, 1981 Commencement Exercise.

3. Letter to Bishop from Senior Citizens, May 5, 1981. Response letter from Bishop Hughes, June 2, 1981.

4.   People such as John Lynch, his uncles, and family, the Purcells; George, his brothers Russell, Joe and Jerry, the Feldman clan; Adolf, his sons Isodore, Francis, and Andrew and their children had helped to start the church and kept it going.

5.   *New York Times Magazine*, "In the Fields of King Coal," by Fenton Johnson, November 22, 1992.

6.   *The Mountain Spirit,* Christian Appalachian Project, Lancaster, Kentucky: November - December 1984, p.5.

7.   Interview with author, June, 1996.

8.   Interview with author, June, 1996.

9.   *Televangelism Power and Politics on God's Frontier*, by Jeffrey K. Hadden and Anson Shupe, Henry Holt and Company, New York: 1988.

10.   Interview with author, June, 1996.

11.   Interview with author, June, 1996.

12.   Interview with author, June, 1996.

13.   Mike Sanders interview with author, April 11, 1996.

14.   Interview with author, April 13, 1996.

15.   Interview with author, June, 1996.

16.   *The Mountain Spirit*, Christian Appalachian Project, Lancaster, Kentucky: September – October, 1982, pp. 5-9.

17.   Ibid.

18.   Interview with author, July, 1996.

19.   Interview with author, July, 1996.

20.   Marilyn Stefanski interview with author, April 13, 1996.

21.   *The Mountain Spirit*, Christian Appalachian Project, Lancaster, Kentucky: January – February, 1986, pp 4-8.

22.   Interview with author, July, 1996.

23.   Interview with author, July, 1996.

24.   Peggy Gabriel interview with author, April 16, 1996.

25.   Interview with author, July, 1996.

26.   *The Messenger*, Covington Diocese Monthly, April 22, 1984.

27.   Interview with author, July, 1996.

28.   *The Mountain Spirit*, Christian Appalachian Project, Lancaster, Kentucky: January – February, 1985, pp. 11-13

29.   Interview with author, July, 1996.

30.   *The Mountain Spirit,* Christian Appalachian Project, Lancaster, Kentucky: January – February, 1985, pp. 14-17.

31.   Rose Price and Donna Turner interview with author, April 11, 1996.

32.   *The Mountain Spirit,* Christian Appalachian Project, Lancaster, Kentucky: July – August 1985, p. 26.

33.   Ibid. May – June, 1986, pp. 16-18.

34.   Interview with author, July, 1996.

35.   Brenda Wireman interview with author, April 11, 1996.

36.   *The Mountain Spirit,* Christian Appalachian Project, Lancaster, Kentucky: March – April, 1996, pgs. 3-9.

37.   Interview with author, July, 1996.

38.   Interview with author, July, 1996.

39.   Mike McLaughlin interview with author, April, 10, 1996.

40. *Unpublished Autobiography of Ministry in Eastern Kentucky*, by Father Ralph Beiting, Feburary 8,1993.

41. *The Mountain Spirit*, Christian Appalachian Project, Lancaster, Kentucky: July – August 1985, p. 20.

42. Ibid., p. 8.

43. Ibid., March – April, 1987, p. 10.

44. Ibid., March – April, 1987, p. 11.

45. *The Georgia Bulletin*, July 16, 1987.

46. Interview with author, July, 1996.

47. *The Record*, Louisville Archdiocesan Newspaper, Louisville, Kentucky: July 16, 1987.

48. Interview with author, July, 1996.

49. *Unpublished Autobiography of Ministry in Eastern Kentucky*, by Father Ralph Beiting, February 8,1993

50. Interview with author, July, 1996.

51. *The Mountain Spirit*, Christian Appalachian Project, Lancaster, Kentucky: September – October, 1988, p.12.

52. Ibid. p.12.

53. Ibid. p. 12.

54. Ibid. p. 13.

55. Interview with author, July, 1996.

56. Interview with author, July, 1996.

57. *The Mountain Spirit*, Christian Appalachian Project, Lancaster, Kentucky: September – October, 1989, p.19.

58. *The Mountain Spirit*, Christian Appalachian Project, Lancaster, Kentucky: January - February, 1985, p.17.

59. Ibid. p. 18.

CHAPTER 8

1. Interview with author, July, 1996.

2. *Perry County News*, Hazard Kentucky, January 4, 1990.

3. Mike Sanders interview with author, April 11, 1996.

4. Interview with author, July, 1996.

5. Interview with author, July, 1996.

6. *Appalachia . . . A Special Place . . . A Bridge of Hope*, by Father Ralph W. Beiting, CAP, Lancaster, Kentucky: 1990, p. 26.

7. Peggy Gabriel interview with author, April, 19, 1996.

8. *The Mountain Spirit*, Christian Appalachian Project, Lancaster, Kentucky: March – April, 1991, pp. 22-26.

9. *Caring People*, Washington, D.C., Volume 3, December, 1990, pp. 14-19.

10. *Promises to Keep*, by Father Ralph W. Beiting, with Tom Pelletier, Christian Appalachian Project, Lancaster, Kentucky: 1991, p.56.

11. Jim Harragan interview with author, April 12, 1996.

12. Interview with author, April 12, 1996.

13. Interview with author, April 14, 1996.

14. *The Messenger*, Covington Diocesan News, June 28, 1992.

15. Interview with author, April 13, 1996.

16. Interview with author, April 13, 1996.

17. The Mountain Spirit, Christian Appalachian Project, Lancaster, Kentucky: May - June, 1992, pp. 4-5.

18. Ibid., pp. 6-8.

19. Interview with author, April 12, 1996.

20. Interview with author, April 12, 1996.

21. With the winning of this award, congratulatory messages came from throughout the United States and other countries.

22. Moe Mercier interview with author, April 10, 1996.

23. Grant Satterly interview with author, April 16, 1996.

24. Satterly letter to author, December 4, 1996.

25. Sheila Helton interview with author, April 10, 1996.

26. Information provided through Human Development Grants program to author, April 10, 1996.

27. Mike McLaughlin interview with author, April 11, 1996.

28. The Mountain Spirit, Christian Appalachian Project, Lancaster, Kentucky: May - June, 1994, p. 15

29. Telephone conversation with author, January 1, 1997.

30. The Mountain Spirit, Christian Appalachian Project, Lancaster, Kentucky: March - April, 1997, p. 10

31. Ibid., January – February, 1997, p.14

32. Interview with author, January 1, 1997.

33. Interview with author, January 1, 1997.

34. The Mountain Spirit, Christian Appalachian Project, Lancaster, Kentucky: May - June, 1997, pp. 20-22

35. Richard Ginn interview with author, April 12, 1997.

36. Rose Price interview with author, April 11, 1997.

37. Letter to author, June 12, 1997.

38. A Time of Crisis . . . A Time for Christ, by Father Ralph W. Beiting with Tom Pelletier, Christian Appalachian Project, Lancaster, Kentucky: 1997.

39. Appalachian Mountain News, Vol. 28, Number 1, Winter, 1998.

40. Interview with author, February 6, 1999.

41. Interview with author, January 1, 1997

EPILOGUE
1. Interviews with author, November 30, December 1, 1996.

2. Father Brinker interview with author, April 19, 1996.

INDEX

INDEX

ABOUT THE PUBLISHER

Incorporated in 1979 for public, charitable, and educational purposes, the Jesse Stuart Foundation is devoted to preserving the legacy of Jesse Stuart, W-Hollow, and the Appalachian way of life. The Foundation, which controls the rights to Stuart's published and unpublished literary works, is currently reprinting many of his best out-of-print books, along with other books which focus on Kentucky and Appalachia.

With control of Jesse Stuart's literary estate—including all papers, manuscripts, and memorabilia—the Foundation promotes a number of cultural and educational programs. It encourages the study of Jesse Stuart's works, and of related material, especially the history, culture, and literature of the Appalachian region.

Our primary purpose is to produce books which supplement the educational system at all levels. We have now produced more than thirty editions and we have hundreds of other regional materials in stock. We want to make these materials accessible to teachers and librarians, as well as general readers. We also promote Stuart's legacy through video tapes, dramas, and presentations for school and civic groups.

Stuart taught and lectured extensively. His teaching experience ranged from the one-room schoolhouse of his youth in eastern Kentucky to the American University in Cairo, Egypt, and embraced years of service as school superintendent, high-school teacher, and high-school principal. "First, last, always," said Jesse Stuart, "I am a teacher. Good teaching is forever and the teacher is immortal."

In keeping with Stuart's devotion to teaching, the Jesse Stuart Foundation is publishing materials that are appropriate for school use. For example, the Foundation has reprinted seven of Stuart's junior books (for grades 3 - 6), and a Teacher's Guide to assist with their classroom use. The Foundation has also published several books that would be appropriate for grades 6 - 12: Stuart's *Hie to the Hunters*, Thomas D. Clark's *Simon Kenton, Kentucky Scout*, and Billy C. Clark's *A Long Row to Hoe*. Other recent JSF publications range from books for adult literacy students to high school and college texts.

Jesse Stuart's books are a guideline to the solid values of America's past. With good humor and brilliant storytelling, Stuart praises the Appalachian people whose quiet lives were captured forever in his wonderful novels and stories. In Jesse's books, readers will find people who value hard work, who love their families, their land, and their country; who believe in education, honesty, thrift, and compassion—people who play by the rules.

ABOUT THE AUTHOR

Dr. Anthony J. Salatino, a native of New York State, came to Appalachia in the early 1960s as Academic Dean of Alice Lloyd College, Pippa Passes, Kentucky. His background is extensive and diverse. He has also served as a University professor and administrator, worked for a major publishing house, and served as CEO for a non-profit organization. Dr. Salatino is an award winning author for the book *Will Appalachia Finally Overcome Poverty?* His great concern for the poor led him to accept the invitation to write this biography of Father Beiting, whom he has admired for giving so much of himself to improve the lives of others.